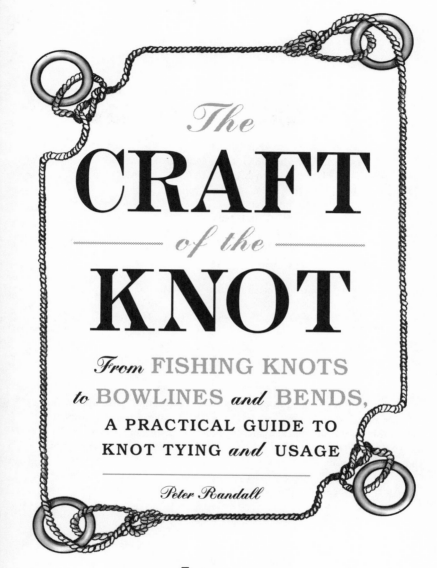

The
CRAFT
of the
KNOT

From FISHING KNOTS
to BOWLINES *and* BENDS,
A PRACTICAL GUIDE TO
KNOT TYING *and* USAGE

Peter Randall

▲**adams**media
Avon, Massachusetts

Published by
Adams Media, a division of F+W Media, Inc.
57 Littlefield Street, Avon, MA 02322. U.S.A.
www.adamsmedia.com

ISBN 10: 1-4405-5249-5
ISBN 13: 978-1-4405-5249-6
eISBN 10: 1-4405-5250-9
eISBN 13: 978-1-4405-5250-2

Printed in the United States of America.

10 9 8 7 6 5 4 3 2 1

Contains material adapted and abridged from *The Everything® Knots Book* by
Randy Penn, copyright © 2004 by F+W Media, Inc., ISBN 10: 1-59337-032-6,
ISBN 13: 978-1-59337-032-9.

Interior illustrations © 123rf.com

This book is available at quantity discounts for bulk purchases.
For information, please call 1-800-289-0963.

CONTENTS

▪▪▪▪▪▪▪▪▪▪▪▪▪▪▪▪▪▪▪▪▪▪▪▪▪▪▪▪▪▪▪▪

THE HISTORY
OF KNOTS

It's said that long ago the ancient kingdom of Phrygia was without a king. Desperate, the kingdom's elders swore that they would take as their ruler the next man to pass through the city gates. It so happened that immediately afterward, a peasant named Gordias drove his ox cart through the gates and was duly hailed by the elders as the new Phrygian king.

Gordias's son, Midas, tethered his father's ox cart to a post near the city's gate. In order that people might remember their ruler's humble origins, Midas tied the cart to the post with a special knot, one that could not be undone by ordinary means. Pulling on it merely made it tighter and firmer. People from far and wide came to marvel at the Gordian Knot, which no one could untie.

Finally, Alexander the Great, the Greek conqueror of Persia, arrived in the city and was shown the knot. Never one to withstand a challenge, Alexander declared that he could undo the Gordian Knot. And while the people of Phrygia watched in amazement—and shock—Alexander drew his sword and sliced through the knot with a single stroke. To this day, when someone has unraveled a particularly difficult problem in a surprising way, we say that they have "cut the Gordian Knot."

Prehistoric Origins

The story of Alexander's feat shows how knots have been woven into the fabric of our history and mythology. Apart from myth, knots have been part of human history as far back as we know—possibly as long ago as 2.5 million years. We can make some educated guesses about the origins of knots and cordage based on the scant traces left of early human lives as well as what we know about that environment, what materials were at hand, and what inspiration was available from the surroundings.

Both plant and animal materials were available to prehistoric humans to be used as cordage. Numerous plants are made of strong fibers that provide structural strength. Some plants—such as vines—can be used as cordage without any preparation at all. Additionally, early hunters had a wide choice of animals as a resource. Hides were cut into thin strips as a ready source of tying materials. Tendons were especially strong. And many other parts of animals have been used throughout the ages.

Early humans must have been inspired to tie their first knots by what they saw around them. Spider webs, bird nests, and even the complex structures of many plants may have given them a hint as to how to proceed. Occasionally small game would become tangled in undergrowth, and even fish would become ensnared in underwater growth. Nature can be a great teacher of what cordage can accomplish.

Some occurrences in the environment probably helped early knot tyers to improve the use of cordage. Perhaps they noticed that when they pulled some twigs apart, two of them would bind if their ends happened to have been bent and overlapped. Plants sometimes grow in Half Hitches around one another. Overhand Knots seem to form spontaneously in cordlike materials. You have, no doubt, seen knots suddenly appear in garden hoses and electrical cords. So, it is not a stretch to imagine that

Overhand Knots, Half Hitches, and various twists in materials could have been tied on purpose in an attempt to duplicate nature.

HISTORICAL EVIDENCE

Ancient artifacts tell us a wide-ranging story about our past. This story has its gaps, especially when it comes to the history of knotting. That is not surprising when you consider that the natural materials cordage was made from decay in almost all environments. However, the surviving samples provide direct evidence of early humans incorporating the technology of knotting into how they lived.

Some of the most direct evidence we have comes from a discovery made by hikers on the Austrian-Italian border in 1991. They came across the mummified body of a human male; carbon dating established that he had died more than 5,300 years before. Ötzi the iceman, as he has become known, carried with him various objects that showed cords and knotting played an important role in his life. His knife was hung by his side by a knotted cord; his sandals were held together with knots (he also had a cloak made of woven grass), as well as his cap, which was secured to his chin with a knotted strap. A bow that he carried must have been strung using knots.

Even when artifacts have no surviving cordage with them, the items can still give us clues that they were used with cordage. For instance, a small decorative jewelry-like item that has a hole cut into it was probably suspended from a cord. Some of the artifacts even show wear at the place where the string would have been tied. Other items have deep indentations that would have needed knotting to hold them in place. Spears and hatchets were shaped to facilitate binding to a shaft. Pottery fragments show indentations of three-strand rope and a surprising variety of decorative knotting. Early artwork in both paintings and carvings also depict knotting.

In more recent times, of course, we have actual pieces of knotting to reveal glimpses of our past. These samples show uses in just about all aspects of life, from decorative objects to hunting-and-gathering instruments. Many cultures have shown ingenuity in making cordage with the materials available; others have truly taken knot tying to an art form.

Signs of Progress

Civilization has come a long way since humans first coaxed fish out of a stream with a woven tangle of vines, but we didn't do it all at once. We accomplished it in many stages, with a steady application of knotting all the way. Whenever humans have learned something new, they have updated the technology of cordage and knotting along with it. For many early users of knots and cordage, being able to tie a line to a fishing hook or lash a spear to a shaft meant being able to feed their family. Being able to make lashings meant building structures to protect the family from the elements. It meant survival. Knot tying was not an optional activity —it was a way of life. Humankind has improved methods for hunting, warring, and surviving the elements, and increased knotting skills went hand in hand with these advances. When it came time to sail the seas, domesticate cattle, and even keep track of numbers and dates, knots continued to be used in new ways.

New cultures, religions, and technologies brought on many changes, and humans learned various new professions. Clothes and blankets take considerable time to tie and weave. When the industrial revolution came along, the first machines made were for tying knots and weaving. Rope had been mass-produced long before then. Through all these changes, few endeavors were taken up without laying in a major supply of cordage.

The existence of knots meant more than just function to our ancestors. As early humans learned to apply symbolism, knots played a key role. Even superstitious beliefs became attached to knots, thereby giving them more than just a symbolic role.

As humankind's use of symbolism and communication developed, knots took on new meaning by way of representation. As people learned to count days, they counted them with knots on a string.

Did you ever wonder how people kept track of meetings before appointment books and smartphones? For some, a bit of string was all that was needed to keep an appointment. Often an invitation to a meeting consisted of a string with a number of knots tied in it to represent the number of days until the event. They would be untied one per day until time was up.

By far the most elaborate record keeping ever done was on knotted strings, or *quipus,* by the Inca of Peru. Each *quipu* was a system of many strands branching off a central cord. The knots on these strands represented all the data needed to administer an empire, including mathematics, census figures, taxes, crops, herds, and many other things. Using knots allowed the Inca to record and calculate data without having a written language.

As humans' imagination and beliefs continued to develop, knots were believed to hold an influence over the things they represented. Early sailors tied knots to symbolize binding the wind within them, and untying them was believed to release the wind. Similar beliefs were held for illness, love, friendship, and political unities. Healers attempted to bind someone's illness within knots, and then release it harmlessly elsewhere.

One Name, Many Knots

The names given to knots provide clues about what they meant to our ancestors. One of the first things you may notice about the names of knots is that some of them refer to professions. From Archer and Bell Ringer to Weaver, knots continue to be called by their namesakes. This implies that they played a key role in these trades.

An important quirk about knotting nomenclature is that some knots have multiple names, and one name can refer to many different knots. When a knot has many different names, it is an indication that, for whatever reason, that knot was significant enough to warrant such attention. Just as there are many words for *snow* in the Eskimo language, important concepts tend to attract multiple labels. When a certain name refers to many different knots, just the opposite can be the case. It can mean that many different knots were used for what the name stood for. A good example of this is the Fisherman's Knot.

Knots of Tomorrow

What has all this history brought us to? Where is it going to take us? For yourself, the answer can only be found with you. Where do you want to be and where do you want to go? For society, the answer is broad and far ranging.

Today some cordage is made out of new synthetic materials, while some is still made of natural fibers. The more slippery of the synthetic materials have made for more careful knot tying, in order to keep the knots themselves from slipping. A vast number of crafts, professions, and activities have brought many new knots into use, each with its own special application and name. Experimenters come up with new knots every day, and ropes of new and different structures even require that splicing be done differently. Decorative knot tyers continue to astound us with their new creations.

However, basic knot tying remains what it has always been—a way to use cordage to help us interact with and control our environment. This is done now and will continue to be done with basic knots that can be readily learned, yet used and shared for a lifetime.

We are tempted to laugh at our past beliefs and superstitions about knots. But the inner workings of knots are just as mysterious today as any time in the past. Many texts refer to the workings of friction, or the key importance of a "nip" in the knot (that particular part of the knot that can be thought of as "locking" it). While not incorrect, in reality these serve mostly as learning aids. Knots put under high strain do not necessarily result in damage at their nip. In fact, they tend to break just outside the knot. The reason for this is not fully understood, and even computer models only seem to confirm this, without explaining why. This is really not surprising, since the science of the late twentieth century has taught us that there can be infinite complexities within even the most simple of systems.

Many avenues of higher learning keep leading us to further research in knots. The higher mathematics of algebraic structures and topology are only beginning to describe knots (there's now a branch of mathematical investigation called "knot theory"). Mathematical progress in classifying knots leads to increased understanding in the mechanics of DNA strands and polymers. It also contributes to the study of higher dimensions and theoretical physics. To be sure, history shall someday lump our current understanding of knots with that of the caveman.

Knots in Your Life

What do you want out of knot tying? One way to tell if you want something is to imagine that you already have it. Simply try to cover the many benefits by highlighting a few specific uses. So, let's suppose that you are well versed in knot tying and can apply a bit of twine or rope to almost any relevant situation.

Let's just name a few of the uses you will have for your new knot-tying knowledge. First of all, congratulations on your tremendous increase in strength, since you now know how to multiply your pulling strength with just a simple Trucker's Hitch. Because this hitch can be tied all the way around something, you can apply a crushing force far beyond the strength you had before you became a knot tyer. Your reach is certainly to be admired, too, especially with your ability to tie both locking and sliding loops in the end of rope.

Do you like to be able to handle emergencies? Thank goodness you are an adept knot tyer. Skill with knots and rope is key to many rescue scenarios, from first aid to evacuations. Do you spend time with children? From simple knots to complex crafts, children the world over enjoy learning about knotting.

If you are the type of person who always likes to keep a tool kit in your car or truck, now you should include some cordage, both big and small. A broken hose clamp is not necessarily a problem for someone who has small cordage and knows the Constrictor Knot.

Knots are no less useful today than they were in ancient times. Modern humans are continuing to find new uses for knots and create new ones. Are you ready to join the ranks of the knot makers?

KNOTTING TERMS

Knowing a few terms for knot tying is very important for following both illustrations and descriptions in the text. When you work with a rope, it generally has a standing part, bight, and running end.

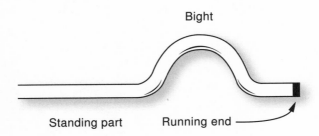

Bight

Standing part   Running end

When a knot is tied at the end of a rope, the very tip is referred to as the "running end." In fishing publications, this section may be referred to as the "tag end." Using this term in knotting directions gives the important distinction that the very tip of the rope is delivered where the directions say, whether it is over or under another rope, or through a loop of some kind. The other end of the rope—the leading part that is not manipulated in the knot tying—is called the "standing part."

The term "bight" is the middle part of the rope that is not the running end or standing part. Just as a running end can be directed in many ways in the construction of a knot, a bight can be made out of any part of the rope, and directed the same way. If an arrow in an illustration seems to come from the standing part and not from the running end, it usually means that a bight should be formed and taken in the direction the arrow shows. It may help with some knots to fold the bight over very tight, thus forming a narrow doubled piece that can pass more easily where needed.

THE CROSSING TURN

Another important structure in knot tying is the crossing turn, used in many of the knots you'll learn in this book. You can quickly create a crossing turn by grabbing a part of the bight and giving it a half twist that forms a loop. When making a crossing turn, it is very important that the orientation of the over-under section of the crossing is correct for the knot you are tying. In practice, you will quickly get the crossing orientation correct each time by associating it with a twist in a certain direction, which is quicker than trying to think about whether the running end crosses over or under when producing it.

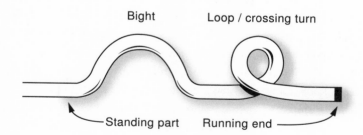

Bight   Loop / crossing turn

Standing part   Running end

Hitching Practices

When you tie a knot in the rope without ever using the running end, you're said to "tie in the bight." Tying in the bight may be done in the middle of the rope or near the end (as long as you're not moving the running end). For example, you can make a Clove Hitch by making two crossing turns in the bight. Then, lay the right crossing turn over the left one, and the resulting hitch can then be placed over the end of a post.

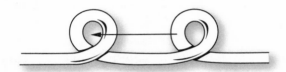

Many knots that are usually tied with the running end can be tied in the bight by folding a bight anywhere in the line and then using it exactly as you would a running end. When a Simple Overhand Knot is tied this way, the bight that protrudes from the knot where the running end would have been can then be used as a loop. This is a good way to make a loop in very small cord or string.

Another term important in understanding knots is *capsizing,* which is when a knot changes its shape due to a rearrangement of one of its parts—for example, when you pull on the knot's loop and it straightens out. If you set up your cord and pull on the running end, it will leave the crossing turn as it straightens and another crossing turn will form on the cord that was running through it. This transformation can happen in knots when they are not snugged down into their proper form, causing the knot to "spill." In the case of the Square or Reef Knot, this is done intentionally, to untie it more quickly (capsizing is sometimes done on purpose to aid in tying a knot).

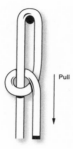

When you're making hitches, you'll also come across "turns" and "round turns." These are two ways of starting a hitch around a ring, bar, or rail. With the turn, the running end is passed just once around the rail, which will allow a transfer of strain from the standing part to the rest of the knot. This may be desirable for some hitches that are better able to hold with strain on them. With the round turn, the extra turn around the rail allows friction to help hold against strain in the standing part, which may help when hitching a rope under strain and takes some of the strain off the knot. The round turn is the first part of the popular hitch called the Round Turn and Two Half Hitches.

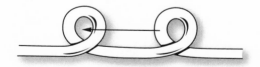

Tying Overhand

The Overhand Knot and the Multiple Overhand Knot structures are used in many knots, and it is valuable to become familiar with their form. The following illustration shows the shape of a Multiple Overhand Knot of three turns in what is called its "belly-and-spine" form (the belly may also be referred to as the bight).

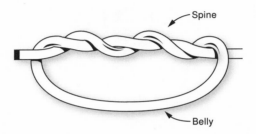

When you tighten the Multiple Overhand Knot by pulling on both ends, the belly wraps around the spine until it is barrel shaped, as shown here.

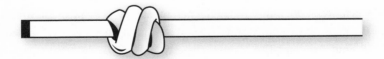

The Best Knot for the Job

When you open a drawer or box of tools, it is immediately obvious that some of them are right and some of them are wrong for the job you have in mind. When you have a job to do with rope, the knots you know will serve you as your toolbox. Just as you would not have much use for a toolbox with just one tool in it, you would not want to do different jobs with rope or string with just one knot. You will want to learn a few different types of knots and learn to use the right one for your application.

The main categories of rope use are joining one rope to another, making a loop, binding, and tying off to an object. Identifying the function that the knot must serve is an important step in choosing one. Some knots are like a multitool in that they can serve a variety of functions, and some are very limited in what they do. A fixed loop will work in several different capacities (for instance, to moor a boat), but a knot like the Reef or Square Knot is unreliable when not used as a binding knot. Once you understand the function of the knot you learn, you will know whether it will work in any particular application.

When choosing a knot for a given application, ask yourself the following questions:

- Will the rope be under steady or changing strain?
- Will it need to be untied?
- Will it need to be tied or untied quickly?
- What knots do I know?
- How secure does it need to be?
- Will others need to tie or untie it?
- Will the tension in the rope need to be adjusted later?
- Will others have to use it?
- Is damaging the rope a concern?

These and many other questions can come into play when you choose a knot. You will, of course, need to limit your choices to which knots you know, just as you must choose from your toolbox only tools that are in it. This leads us to another question you may have been wondering about: "Which knots should I learn?"

CHOOSING WHICH KNOTS TO LEARN

Many people are quite intimidated by the thought of learning more than just a couple of knots, or think that it is difficult or time-consuming. So here are some things to ponder when deciding which ones you want to learn.

The first thing you may wonder about is how many knots you will need to know or what is the smallest number that you can get by on. The number is up to you and may vary depending on your needs. Here is a possible progression you might consider: A loop knot like the Bowline or Overhand Loop can serve a number of different applications, and thus gets you the most mileage from a single knot. Next you should consider learning other knots from different categories, like bends, hitches, and binding knots, so that you can apply them to many situations. It is better still to learn a couple of knots from each category. You might try experimenting with a number of knots within a given category, and settle on the ones you want to remember and use.

Many knots are similar in structure, which means that the more different kinds of knots you learn to make, the easier it'll be to add new knots to your stock. Because of this, you may decide to choose knots from different categories that have similar structure—you'll be able to remember them more easily. For example, the multiple overhand structure appears in many knots throughout this book, and so do knots that make use of combinations of Half Hitches.

Taking time to study knot-tying tips and terminology is key to success at learning new knots. Knot-tying practice also helps in following diagrams and in mastering successively complex knots more easily. With a little work, you will have no trouble both tying and teaching many of the different knots in this book. The chapters that follow include many types of knots, and even tips on teaching them and exploring the subject further.

PART I

KNOT STYLES

Chapter 1

SIMPLE STOPPERS

The best place to start learning knots is with stopper knots, or knots that are tied at the end of a cord. Stopper knots have many uses and provide an excellent learning base for practicing a wide variety of other knots.

STOPPING AND MORE

Stopper knots, also known as terminal knots or knob knots, are tied at the end of a cord. In its strictest sense, the use of the word knot refers to a stopper knot.

A rope with a knot tied in the end of it is a completely different object than a rope without one. It is easier to hang on to, it cannot be pulled through the same size openings, the end will be less inclined to come unraveled, and it will look different, too. All these changes in the properties of the rope are accomplished with a simple stopper knot.

Basic Usage

To stop a cord's end from running through a small opening is part of how a stopper knot earns its name. By "stopping" the rope, the knot allows us to suspend something from it. If the cord runs through a lead or pulley, a stopper knot can keep the line from running all the way out, or unreeving. This is commonly done on a sailboat, where the Figure Eight Knot is used for this purpose. It also stops the end of thread from passing through cloth and similar materials in needlework.

A simple stopper knot is often used to make cordage easier to grasp, whether you make it with the string doubled through the end of a zipper, or with larger rope to get a better grip. Several stopper knots can be tied, and spaced out, to give many handholds. When tied in the ends of many cords as if all one cord, it provides a way to keep them gathered.

What's It Used For?

There are many other uses for stopper knots. They can make the end heavier to use for throwing. Heaving knots are for weighting the end of a rope to assist with throwing the rope. Often a smaller rope is thrown between a boat and the dock, and then used to pull a heavier one over. The same technique is used in many circumstances to get a heavy rope in a hard-to-reach place. In getting a rope over and between two particular branches high in a tree, a rope can be thrown over all of them, and then another can be thrown across it between the branches, from a different angle, 90 degrees if possible. In this manner, the second rope will pull the first down between the two branches. Two common knots for weighting the end of a line are the Heaving Line Knot and the Monkey's Fist.

Stopper knots can be used as mallets with a soft striking surface, or they can be treated with shellac to harden them. They also use up line to make it shorter. Both the Heaving Line Knot and the Monkey's Fist have a number of turns that use up line. Depending on how much shorter a cord needs to be, anything can be used from an Overhand Knot to a long Heaving Line Knot or even a coil. They can prevent the end from fraying, although whipping the end, as shown in Appendix A, is a neater solution. Stopper knots are used for decoration, and a knot in the end of a cord can be used as a reminder of something.

MULTISTRAND STOPPER KNOTS

Knot tyers long ago figured out that the strands of three-stranded rope can be unlayed and then tied together to form simple or complex stopper knots. These knots are characterized by simple and easy-to-remember patterns for tying, and their woven appearance. On square-rigged sailing ships these knots were used to stop hands and feet from sliding on ropes. They can also be tied by binding two or more separate cords together. Multistrand knots are also used as a form of decorative knot tying. Some knots, like the Matthew Walker Knot, can serve both decorative and functional purposes.

Multistrand stopper knots can be made in many variations just by using the Wall and Crown Knots (described later in this chapter). They can be combined in various orders and can even be doubled to make a larger knot. To double them, retrace each strand along a previous strand's path. If a Wall and then a Crown is made, the ends can be tucked down the center from the top and then cut off where they come out the bottom. Then, when someone asks what you did with the ends, you can say that you "threw them away."

The Overhand Series

The Overhand Knot is a distinct knot with its own properties. It is also the basis for both tying and remembering many knots. For instance, the Overhand Knot is the base for two important series of stopper knots, the figure eight series and the multiple overhand series.

Overhand Knot

STEP 1   Pass the running end around the standing part, making a loop, and then pass it through the crossing turn.

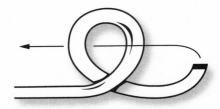

STEP 2 Tighten the knot by pulling on both the standing part and the running end.

Besides being the foundation of many different knots, the Overhand Knot has many distinct properties of its own. For example, it weakens most cordage it is tied in by 50 percent or more, and tightening it down can damage the fibers of some ropes. Consequently, it is tied in nylon fishing line to test for brittleness. If fishing line has lost any of its flexibility, it will break very easily as you tie an Overhand Knot in it and tighten it with a quick jerk from both sides. Fishermen take care not to accidentally let an Overhand Knot form in their line so as not to lose half its strength. Once it's tied, the knot is difficult to undo. It should only be tied in small cordage or thread if it is not meant to be untied.

THE FIGURE EIGHT SERIES

The figure eight series contains frequently used knots. This series begins by making the crossing turn that would be used for an Overhand Knot, and then increasing the number of times the running end is wrapped around the standing part before passing once through the loop. Twisting this loop an increasing number of times before threading accomplishes the same thing. This series of knots is often used to stop a line from passing through an opening.

FIGURE EIGHT KNOT

This knot is started like the Overhand Knot, but here the running end makes a complete round turn around the standing part before passing through its loop.

STEP 1   Use the running end to make a crossing turn, and pass the end under the standing part.

STEP 2   Twist the running end up and through the crossing turn.

STEP 3 Tighten the knot by pulling on both ends.

If you wish to use the Figure Eight Knot as a stopper knot, modify Step 2 by pulling the standing part while pressing against the base of the knot on that side. When the Figure Eight Knot and similar stopper knots are tightened this way, the running end will point to the side at a right angle.

The Figure Eight Knot is frequently used as a basis for other knots. It is much easier to untie than the Overhand Knot, and is not as damaging to rope fibers. Because the Figure Eight Knot has a distinctive "figure eight" look, it's easy to check to make sure it's tied correctly. This is one of the reasons it is popular with rescue work. It is used on the running rigging of sailboats to keep lines from running all the way through leads and pulleys.

THE MULTIPLE OVERHAND SERIES

The multiple overhand series is made by increasing the number of wraps in the spine of the knot. After making an Overhand Knot, pass the running end through the loop of the knot multiple times, making a different knot in the series every time.

When tied this way, these knots change shape as they are tightened. If you tighten them by pulling on both the running and standing parts, the belly wraps around the spine until all you can see is the barrel shape of these wraps. They can also be tightened by manually wrapping the belly around the spine, which causes the spine to unwrap to a single crossing. These knots have many properties in common, including both high security and difficulty in untying when tightened.

Another way to tie this series is to make the desired number of wraps, and then pass the running end through all of them, leaving it already in its final form. The Double and Triple Overhand Knots are often tied this way. Knots of this series all have a right- and a left-handed version.

These knots are also sometimes called Barrel Knots or Blood Knots—the latter possibly because they were tied to the lashes of a cat-o'-nine-tails to help the flogger draw more blood from his victim. Another version claims the name comes from causing bleeding fingers from tight knots in fishing lines.

WHERE TO START?

Knots in the overhand series are the starting points of many other knots, bends, hitches, and loops. Some bends are made by interlocking Overhand Knots, some hitches are started with an Overhand or Figure Eight, and many friction loops and fishing knots are based on Multiple Overhand Knots.

For the series of stopper knots mentioned here, increasing the number of wraps will not increase their cross-section area. For a wider knot, use a different knot or double the cord first.

There are many advantages to tying knots that are based on others. They are certainly easier to remember because there is so much less to recall. By making it easier to keep many possibilities in mind, you can make better choices for what is needed. When one knot is the basis for another, it is also easier to check your progress as you complete the knot.

BACK SPLICE

To make a Back Splice, you need to prepare the rope by adding temporary binding where the strands separate out. This is where you will begin making the knot.

STEP 1   Begin the Back Splice by tying a Crown Knot (see following).

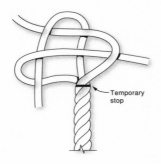

Temporary
stop

STEP 2   Take the first strand and tuck in an over-and-under sequence.

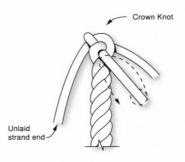

Crown Knot

Unlaid
strand end

STEP 3 Continue tucks for a minimum of three times.

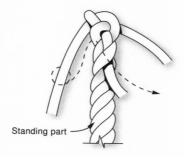

Standing part

STEP 4 When you finish, you should have a rope end that looks like this.

Tuck

The Back Splice Knot is used to keep three-strand rope from fraying and coming apart. If desired, the strands can be partially trimmed after each tuck to taper the splice.

CROWN KNOT

The Crown Knot is very similar to the Wall Knot (see further), except the direction of the running ends, which go down rather than up.

STEP 1 Take the three strands of the rope and tuck each one down through the loop made by another strand.

STEP 2 Tighten the knot by pulling on the strands.

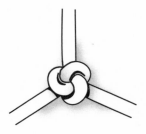

This knot is rarely tied by itself, unless you keep on tying this knot to cover a cylindrical object.

DOUBLE OVERHAND KNOT

This knot is the first in the multiple overhand series. It starts with a Simple Overhand Knot, and then the running end is passed through the crossing turn a second time, making the belly-and-spine appearance you see in Step 1.

STEP 1 Lay down the rope with the running end facing left. Move it down and twist to make the belly, bringing it up over the right side of the standing part.

STEP 2 Run the running end up and under the standing part, making two overhand loops.

STEP 3 Tighten the knot by pulling on both the standing part and the running end.

Twisting the ends in opposite directions will either help the belly wrap around the spine or impede it, depending on which way they are twisted. The Double Overhand, like all knots in the series, is very secure and difficult to untie.

Matthew Walker Knot

This is another decorative knot that requires separating the rope you're working with into three strands.

STEP 1 Begin the Matthew Walker Knot by making a Wall Knot (see further), tucking each end up through the next bight.

STEP 2 Continue by making another tuck.

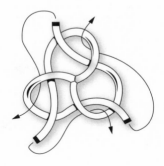

STEP 3 Snug down by pulling each of the strands repeatedly.

Another way to tie the Matthew Walker Knot is to lay the strands in successive Overhand Knots.

STEP 1 Use one strand to make an Overhand Knot.

STEP 2 Continue making Overhand Knots with each consecutive strand.

As you pull on the strands to tighten the knot, make sure you do it gradually and evenly. The outer bights must be coaxed into place to wrap around the knot in the proper form. Gently brush them with your hand to assist them in wrapping all the way around the knot, while gradually and evenly taking out slack.

MONKEY'S FIST

The Monkey's Fist Knot is most frequently used as a heaving knot, and can even be tied around an object to make it heavier. The knot is also popular with children and is used as a decorative knot (see Chapter 11 for more on decorative knots). It is made small to give earrings a nautical look, larger to make key fobs, and larger still to make doorstops. A pair tied to opposite ends of a two-foot cord makes a good cat toy.

Before you start making the knot, estimate the length of line needed by making nine or ten loops of about the size that will be tied.

STEP 1 Make the initial set of three vertical turns.

STEP 2 Hold the turns in place as you add three horizontal turns.

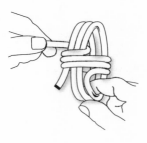

STEP 3 Next, add three turns that go through the middle of the knot, wrapping over the top and around the vertical turns.

STEP 4 Take care that the loops stay in place, and that they continue to stay in place, as you carefully work the slack out through the knot, one turn at a time.

The end can be left long and spliced into the standing part, or tucked into the knot. If the end is to be tucked within the knot, an Oysterman's Stopper (see Chapter 6) tied in the end will help fill its center. After it is pushed into the middle of the knot, work the slack back to the standing part of the cord.

A variation on the Monkey's Fist Knot is to use more than three turns. And for the ambitious knot tyer, a three-turn Monkey's Fist can serve as the center for a five-turn Monkey's Fist, and so forth, tucking each Monkey's Fist inside the new one such that lines stay perpendicular.

The Monkey's Fist can be dangerous if it hits a bystander while throwing it. Sometimes a small bag of sand is used to weight the end of a line if there is a risk of injury.

SLIPPED FIGURE EIGHT KNOT

If you want your Figure Eight Knot to release quickly, modify it by making it into a Slipped Figure Eight Knot. This knot is tied from a different version of the Figure Eight Knot.

Use the running end to make a crossing turn by twisting the end down and over the standing part and underneath it. Then, use the bight of the running end to pull it through the loop.

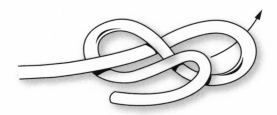

You can release this knot simply by pulling on the running end.

TRIPLE OVERHAND KNOT

This next knot in the multiple overhand series is tied similarly to the Double Overhand, but with three passes through the loop instead of two. When tied this way, it also has the belly-and-spine appearance you see in Step 1.

STEP 1 Tying this knot, you follow the steps described in the Double Overhand Knot (see previous), adding an extra loop at the end.

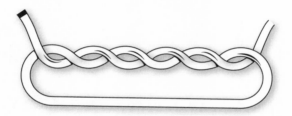

STEP 2 When you pull on both ends to tighten the knot, the belly will wrap around the spine, giving the knot its final barrel shape when fully tightened.

STEP 3 A popular way to tie this knot is to make the wraps working backward along the standing part, and then passing the running end through all the wraps at once.

WALL KNOT

Generally, the Wall Knot is not tied on its own, but is the basis for other knots, such as the Wall and Crown Knot, which is made by first tying a Wall and then a Crown Knot (see previous). A continuous set of Wall Knots can cover a cylindrical object.

STEP 1   In order to make the Wall Knot, you'll need to separate the end of the rope into three strands. Each of the strands is tucked upward through the loop made by another strand.

STEP 2 Tighten the knot by pulling on the strands.

In preparing three-strand rope for multistrand knots, it is best to whip the end of each strand and bind the rope itself with a Constrictor Knot (see Chapter 6) to keep the strands from separating any further down the rope.

Chapter 2

BASIC BENDS

A knot used to join the ends of two ropes is called a bend. The knots you will find in this chapter will join cordage small and large, similar and different—a skill that you will find useful in many endeavors.

When a bend joins the ends of two ropes, it is to provide more length or make a needed connection. A bend should be considered a temporary join, except in the case of small cordage such as twine or fishing line. You may need a bend to repair a broken rope (keeping in mind that rope is weaker at the knot). You can use a bend to join electrical cords. When the ends are plugged in, they will not pull out if there is tension on the cord.

Before working with electrical cords, be sure the electric current to them is turned off.

When used to join the ends of a single rope, a bend makes a circle of rope called a "strop" or "sling." A closed circle of rope can be used for hitching or lifting, such as the Barrel Sling described in Chapter 4.

Bends are characterized by having two standing ends and two running ends. When tightened down, leave enough length of running end to provide security against the ends slipping back through the knot. Depending on the knot, the length of the running end can be anywhere from a few to several times the diameter of the rope. If extra security is desired, the running ends can even be tied around the standing ends of the opposite rope. You can use anything from a Half Hitch to a Triple Overhand Knot for this purpose.

Bends vary in how easily they are untied after being under strain. Since ease of untying may or may not be desirable depending on your circumstances, you want to keep this property in mind when you choose your bend. Knots like the Water Knot or the Fisherman's Knot can be very difficult to untie, especially in twine. The Zeppelin Bend can be untied easily even after being subjected to great strain.

It often happens that the ropes you want to join will be of different size or material. Take great care because most bends have very little security when they are not tied with two identical ropes. There are two ways of dealing with this. One is to use a knot that is somewhat suited for ropes of different sizes, such as the Sheet Bend or the Double Sheet Bend, and the other is to treat the join as if it were a hitch.

The Sheet Bend is commonly used when a rope of larger size is tied to a smaller one. In this case, the larger cord is the one that is bent into a U-shape, as you'll see in the instructions for tying the Sheet Bend later in this chapter. If the size difference is too large, however, this knot will be insecure. To help the join handle a bigger size difference, you can use a Double Sheet Bend. These knots are also popular for ropes that are of different material. For each circumstance, you must tie and test your join to determine its suitability.

When the size difference of the ropes to be joined is significant, you may not want to tie them together at all, but connect them with loops or hitches. A rope can also be tied to a larger rope with a hitch just as if it were a pole. This is made easier if there is a loop at the end of the larger rope to which a smaller rope can be attached with almost any hitch. A loop can also be tied in each end so that they interlock. The Bowline Bend is such a join and if the loop knots themselves are secure, this join is secure regardless of the differences of the two ropes.

INTERLOCKING OVERHAND BENDS

A type of joining knot worth learning is the Interlocking Overhand Bend. In this type of knot, the end of each rope forms an Overhand Knot, and they are intertwined. Out of the many different joining knots that can be made from Interlocking Overhand Knots, four are shown in this chapter: Ashley's Bend, Hunter's Bend, Zeppelin Bend, and Butterfly Bend. These are all excellent bends, each with its own properties and tying methods.

There are two approaches to tying Interlocking Overhand Knots. One is to tie an Overhand Knot in one end, and then tie an Overhand in the other end while threading this end through the first Overhand. The other method is to ignore the fact that the ends make an Overhand Knot, and just intertwine both ends as needed to make the knot. This is illustrated for each of these four knots in this chapter, along with a figure showing the overhand structure of each.

You should try a number of the knots in this chapter before deciding which ones best serve your needs. Some work better with smaller or larger cordage, some tie more quickly and easily than others, and some are easier to untie. In some, the running ends lead out the side of the knot. In others, they lie along the standing parts. While some will be fun to tie, others may be too cumbersome. Whatever your preferences, the only way you will find out what you like is by trying out all these bends.

Ashley's Bend

This knot is named after Clifford W. Ashley, who first introduced it in his book, *The Ashley Book of Knots*.

STEP 1 Take the first cord and make a crossing turn.

STEP 2 Take the second cord and use it to lace another crossing turn through the first cord.

STEP 3 Form the final tuck by bringing both running ends through the center together.

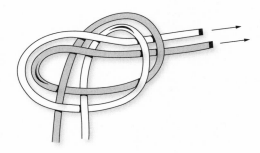

STEP 4 Tighten down the cord, forming Ashley's Bend.

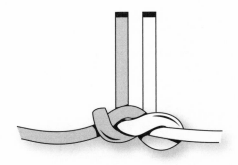

Ashley's Bend is very strong and secure when used to join similar ropes. It does not slip even when brought under severe shock loads, but can be untied easily when desired.

Backing Up Bend

You can make a bend more secure by tying down the running ends. Backing Up is a good method for bends like the Surgeon's Bend, where running ends exit parallel to the standing parts.

Tie down the running ends of a Surgeon's Bend (see further) with a Half Hitch (see Chapter 4) on each side.

This extra tie-off can also be an Overhand Knot. When you make bends with climbing rope, you may also consider using Triple Overhand Knots (see Chapter 1) as a backup—the extra tie-off will make the knot safer and will keep the running ends of the knot from waving around.

BOWLINE BEND

If it happens that two ropes that need to be joined are greatly dissimilar in size or material—or both—a bend may not be a safe and secure solution. Instead, what you can do is join the two ropes by forming two loops. If a loop is tied in one end, and a loop is tied in the other end so that it passes through the first one, then together they make a bend. If both loops are Bowlines, then the result is called a Bowline Bend.

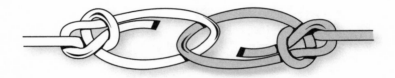

Here are two interlocking Bowline Loops.

BUTTERFLY BEND

Also called the Straight Bend, this knot has the same form as the Butterfly Loop (see Chapter 3), and can even be tied the same way if the ends are attached.

STEP 1 Place two ropes side by side—one on the right and one on the left—and cross the running ends, forming loops.

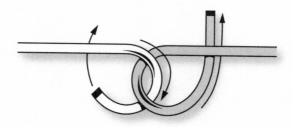

STEP 2 Use the right-side cord's running end to make a second loop.

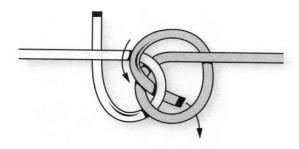

STEP 3 Use the left-side cord's running end to make its second loop as well.

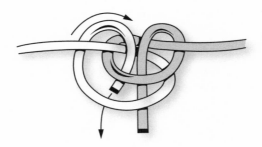

STEP 4 Tighten down the knot by pulling apart the two standing parts and tugging down the running ends.

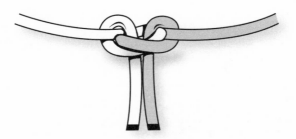

You can also tie the Butterfly Bend by tucking both ends at once, holding one in each hand. It is quicker than it sounds. Use the Butterfly Bend to tie similar materials. It is strong, secure, and unties easily.

CARRICK BEND

The Carrick Bend is traditionally used on large ropes, such as ships' hawsers. When it has been under strain and perhaps wet, it is loosened by striking the outer bights of the knot with something blunt, like a wooden fid (an object like a marlinespike).

STEP 1 Lay down two ropes, one on the left and one on the right. Use the running end of the rope on the right to make a crossing turn. Take the other rope and move its running end in an over-and-under pattern through the right-hand rope.

STEP 2 Finish the tuck.

STEP 3 Pull on both standing ends, and take slack out with the running ends as well.

Because of its symmetrical shape before it is tightened down, the Carrick Bend is also tied for many decorative applications.

DOUBLE SHEET BEND

Another version of the Sheet Bend is the Double Sheet Bend, which you may prefer for use with two ropes that come in different sizes, or if you require a more secure bend.

STEP 1   Start by making a Sheet Bend (see further). Pass the running end around the knot again to tuck under its standing part a second time, making two wraps.

STEP 2   Tighten the Double Sheet Bend.

The Double Sheet Bend can be used to tie a rope to a clothlike material or the top of a sack, if the flat material is used as the end that is folded over.

Hunter's Bend

Although most knots don't result in publicity, this knot did when Dr. Richard Hunter brought it to public attention, leading to the formation of the International Guild of Knot Tyers in 1982. Today, this knot is also called the Rigger's Bend.

STEP 1 Start by placing the two ropes together, with the running ends facing opposite directions.

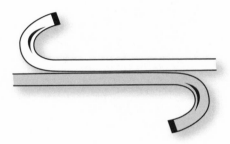

STEP 2 Use both ropes to make a crossing turn.

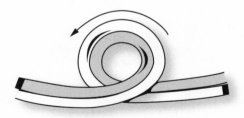

STEP 3 Tuck the running ends through the turn in opposite directions.

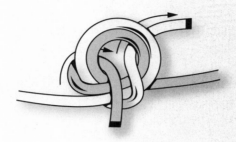

STEP 4 Tighten by taking out slack with both the standing parts and the running ends.

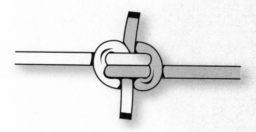

If you use two identical ropes to tie the Hunter's Bend, it will hold well and securely. Another benefit of this knot is that it unties readily.

OVERHAND BEND

The Overhand Bend is quick to tie and is best used with small cordage like thread or string. It is secure, but makes a connection that is only half as strong as the material it is tied in.

STEP 1   Place two ends of the cord or two cords next to each other, and use the double cord to tie an Overhand Knot.

STEP 2 Tighten by pulling the standing parts in opposite directions.

The Overhand Bend is also tied as a decorative way to combine a couple of loose ends. It can also be used to gather a large number of strands by just laying them all together and tying an Overhand Knot with all of them, though this use would be more like a binding knot in function.

SHEET BEND

The Sheet Bend is widely used and is of the same structure as the Bowline Bend (see previous), but with the leads performing a different function. Consider the two ropes you need to join for this bend. If one of the ropes is larger, it should be used for the end that is folded over double.

STEP 1 Take two pieces of rope. Take the rope on the left and make a loop, with the running end facing upward. Then, take the rope on the right and move the running end up between the loop and around the back of the other rope.

STEP 2 Continue the tuck by moving the running end down and through the loop, under itself.

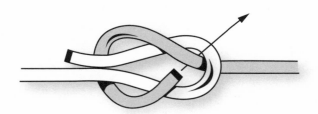

STEP 3 Tighten the bend by pulling the slack out of the running end, and then pulling on the standing parts.

If the size difference between the two ropes is too much, or if the tying materials are slippery, the Double Sheet Bend (see previous) may provide more security.

SLIPPED SHEET BEND

This bend is a modified version of the Sheet Bend (see previous). In this particular bend, the last tuck is made with a bight instead of a single running end.

STEP 1   Follow Step 1 for tying the Sheet Bend. As you move to Step 2, double up the running end and use the bight to move through the loop and under itself.

STEP 2   You can also tie a Slipped Bend by taking an extra turn around the knot before tucking the bight.

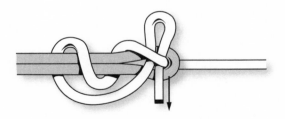

The Slipped Sheet Bend is at least as secure as the regular Sheet Bend, but with the added convenience of having quick release. The alternate slipknot shown in Step 2 can be useful when there is a larger difference in rope sizes.

Surgeon's Bend

When the Surgeon's Knot is used to join two ropes, it can be called the Surgeon's Bend. (To learn how to tie a Surgeon's Knot, see Chapter 10.)

STEP 1 Start by passing one rope's running end over the other, making two passes.

STEP 2 Pull up the two running ends and pass one over the other, making a half knot.

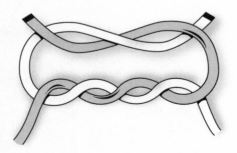

When tightened down, this bend has a unique low-profile shape, which you can see in the previous illustration of the Backing Up Bend. The Surgeon's Bend is secure in most materials, and relatively easy to untie.

WATER KNOT

The Water Knot is a strong knot that holds well with straps or flat webbing.

STEP 1   Tie an Overhand Knot in the end of one rope, then take a second rope and trace it through the knot in the opposite direction.

STEP 2   Continue tracing along the reverse path until both ropes form the Overhand Knot.

STEP 3 Tighten the knot by pulling on both ends.

The Water Knot is difficult to untie after being under strain. If you use flat material to tie this knot, be careful that the straps don't make a twist inside the knot, but that they lay down flat together, as in Step 3.

ZEPPELIN BEND

The Zeppelin Bend, also known as the Rosendahl Bend, is a good sailing bend to learn.

STEP 1   To start, place two ropes together and use one of the running ends to make a loop as shown in the illustration.

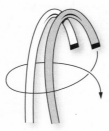

STEP 2   Next, separate the standing parts, moving one of them (the one at the end of the rope that did not form the loop) under the looped running end and over the other running end.

STEP 3   Use the same rope's running end to make the final tuck.

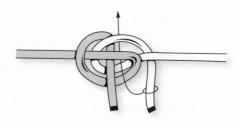

STEP 4   Tighten down the knot, leaving short running ends to stick out perpendicular to the ropes.

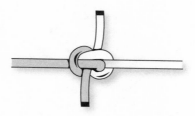

The Zeppelin Bend is very strong and secure when used to join similar ropes. It unties easily even after being under great strain.

Interlocking Overhand Bends

Four of the bends in this chapter—Ashley's Bend, Butterfly Bend, Hunter's Bend, and Zeppelin Bend—consist of Interlocking Overhand Knots. Although each of these knots can be tied without reference to their overhand structures, they are illustrated here for the sake of the completeness of these very superb bends. As you can see in the following illustration, an Overhand Knot has three internal openings that can interlock with other knots. Making an Overhand Knot at the end of one rope and then interlacing another Overhand through it can tie any of these bends.

A right-handed Overhand Knot

Hunter's Bend

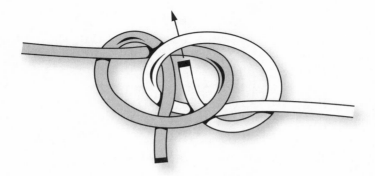

Ashley's Bend

Zeppelin Bend

Butterfly Bend

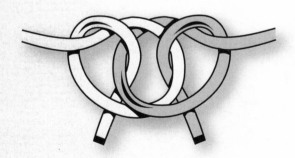

Can you see the Interlocking Overhand Knots in each one of these bends?

Chapter 3

EASY LOOPS

A rope with a loop tied in it is a completely different tool than one without a loop. The majority of tasks you will ever do with rope or string can be done or aided by tying a loop in it.

As the most versatile knot you can tie, a loop can function in any category of knot, including a stopper knot, hitch, part of a bend, and even as binding or decoration. A loop can be used as a hitch either by tying and then passing the loop over the end of an object, or by first passing the end around an object and then tying. Two interlocking loops can be used to fasten one rope to another, thereby making a reliable bend.

There are many different loop knots to choose from. You can tie a loop at the end of a rope or in the middle. It can slide like a noose or be locked in place, or even have multiple turns.

A locked fixed loop does not slide and keeps its size when strain is placed on it. Once a locked loop is tied, it can be thrown over a peg or hook to secure the rope, and then lifted off and used again. If tied for a handhold or around your waist, it will not close down on you. The Bowline Loop is probably the most well-known of this form. Some locked loops are made by splicing a three-stranded rope and using the strands to tie the loop.

When you need more than one loop, you can tie a knot with multiple loops. Complexly shaped objects can be hoisted without tilting, and a single rope can be fastened to multiple anchor points. Loops can even be different sizes. If you need a large number of custom-sized loops for hoisting or binding, you can start with a small fixed loop with a large running end left over. Repeatedly make your loops with the running end, passing it through the locked loop each time, tying off the last one.

You may need a loop that is adjustable in size. Sliding loops, also called nooses or slip loops, fill this purpose. Fishermen often want a loop that will hold its shape until just enough pressure is put on it, causing it to pull down with a jerk that sets a hook in a fish. Sometimes you just want your loop to fit something snugly, but need to tie it ahead of time. If you have a fixed loop and need to make it larger, you can just pull a bight of the standing part through the loop, giving you as large of a loop as needed. An example of this is the Running Bowline.

There is a world of loop knots to choose from, and even if you prefer to remember just one locked loop, you can make a sliding loop or a multiple loop from it. Loop knots are rewarding to learn and tie, and rope becomes quite a diverse tool when you learn them.

Bowline Loop

Commonly referred to as the "Bowline," this loop knot has been in such widespread use that it is also referred to as the "king of knots." It is still in much use today, and with a little caution can be used in the newer synthetic materials.

STEP 1 Make a crossing turn.

STEP 2 Bring the running end up through it, and then behind the standing part.

STEP 3 Twist the running end all the way around the standing part and back down through the crossing turn.

STEP 4 Take out all the slack to make the loop secure. As you tighten the knot, make sure you pull on all the leads.

STEP 5   You can also tie the Bowline Loop with an extra hitch, especially if you want to increase security.

There's another way of tying the Bowline—by laying the running end down across the standing part. It's a quicker start, and you can tie the loop one-handed.

If you want the Bowline Loop to be quick release, try the Slipped Bowline instead by making the last tuck with a bight.

The Bowline Knots are secure, but to maximize safety, make sure you leave at least twelve diameters' length of running end after the knot is tightened, and tie the loop with an extra hitch, as shown in Step 5.

BUTTERFLY LOOP

Also called the Alpine Butterfly, this loop is strong, secure, and easily untied after being put under strain. It's a great loop for use anywhere along a rope, and holds well even with strain put on both standing parts.

STEP 1   Twist the rope twice to make two adjacent crossing turns.

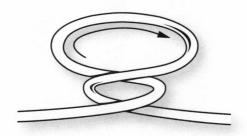

STEP 2   Pull down the outer turn.

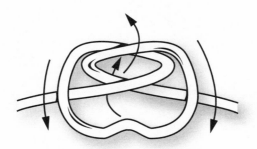

STEP 3   Bring the middle of the loop up through the center of the other crossing turn.

To tighten the loop, pull on all the leads. As you can see, the Butterfly Loop ties very quickly with just a little practice.

Directional Figure Eight

The Directional Figure Eight is an excellent loop that can be tied in the end of a rope to be used as a fixed loop, or anywhere in the middle where the pull will be along the direction of the rope.

STEP 1   Start by making a bight, then fold it back along one side.

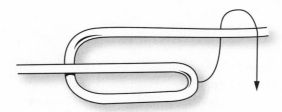

STEP 2   Pass the bight behind the standing part and back under the first crossing turn, exactly in the manner of making a Figure Eight.

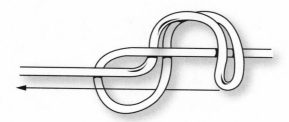

STEP 3   As you tighten the knot, the final loop will lay in the direction that strain will be placed on it.

The Directional Figure Eight can be tied so that the loop points right or left. The steps illustrated here result in a left-pointing loop. To tie a right-pointing one, start the first tuck in the opposite direction. A good rule of thumb to remember is that you start the first tuck in the opposite direction from which you want the loop to lay.

DOUBLE BOWLINE

The Double Bowline is similar to the Bowline Loop, but it's started with a double crossing turn.

STEP 1   Start with a double crossing turn.

STEP 2   Finish the knot just like a regular Bowline (see previous).

Also called the Round Turn Bowline, this version can provide for more security, especially if the rope used is very slippery.

Figure Eight Loop

The Figure Eight Loop is popular with climbers due to its distinctive look when tightened, which helps to determine whether it is tied correctly. For a high level of security, the running end can be secured to the standing part with a Triple Overhand Knot (see Chapter 1).

STEP 1 Begin by folding over the running end to make a bight, and use it to form a Figure Eight.

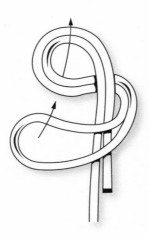

STEP 2   As you tighten the knot, the bight will form the loop.

Strong and secure, the Figure Eight Loop can also be tied around an object by making a regular Figure Eight Knot (see Chapter 1), leaving enough running end to bring around the object and then back to trace through the Figure Eight toward the standing part.

Overhand Loop

The Overhand Loop is a very common way of tying a loop. It's quick to tie and is especially useful with very small cordage like thread or string. It is difficult to untie after being under strain, so it is usually used when it is not meant to be untied.

STEP 1   Begin by folding over the running end to make a bight.

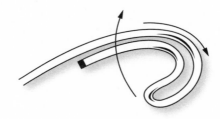

STEP 2   Tie the bight in an Overhand Knot, forming the Overhand Loop.

Note that the Overhand Loop can be tied near the running end or in the bight. If a Double Overhand is tied instead of a single one, it makes an excellent loop for string or fishing line.

Triple Crown Loop

The Triple Crown Loop Knot is much easier to learn if you have tied the Crown Knot found in Chapter 1, the chapter on stopper knots.

STEP 1 Start with a bight, separate the end into two bights, and lay the standing part over one of them, making the first part of the crown.

STEP 2 Fold the right side of the loop over the standing part.

STEP 3 Fold left side of the loop over the right one and through the crossing turn.

STEP 4 Pull the standing part and both loops evenly to get the final form.

Strong and secure, the two loops of the Triple Crown Loop Knot can take strain independently. If the knot is tied close to the end, tie off the shorter standing part to the longer one with a knot of your choice—it will make the knot more secure. After tying the Triple Crown Loop, you can turn it over and crown it again if you like.

TRIPLE FIGURE EIGHT

This loop is similar to the Figure Eight Loop, demonstrated earlier in this chapter. To start, you'll need to fold over the end of the rope, forming a long bight.

STEP 1   Use the doubled-up rope to start tying a Figure Eight Loop.

STEP 2   Pull through a bight of the doubled line.

STEP 3   Take the loop end and wrap it around the top, and then tuck it back down with the other loops.

It will take a little practice to get a feel for how much line to use. Each of the three loops can be made a different size. Climbers use this knot to belay or fasten a line to three anchor points.

Chapter 4

PRACTICAL HITCHES

When you need to attach a rope to an object, the knot for this job is called a "hitch." This is a common use for rope and you will find a variety of hitches in this chapter that will do a good job.

Hitches allow you to secure a rope to rings, rails, posts, hooks, other ropes, and other objects. Sometimes they are tied by forming the knot directly around the object, and sometimes by bringing the rope around the object and tying the running end to the standing part. If the shape of the object allows it, you can tie the hitch (or a loop) first, and then place it around the object. Some hitches, like the Rolling Hitch or Icicle Hitch, provide a friction grip to prevent them from sliding when strain is along the direction of the pole, rail, or rope.

You may want tension to remain in the rope after the hitch is tied. If you are frustrated by a little slack going into the rope as the hitch is tightened, you will find that making an extra wrap around the object, called "making a round turn," will help hold tension as the knot is tied. An example of this is the Round Turn and Two Half Hitches. Another option is to tie a hitch that allows you to take out slack repeatedly without untying the hitch itself, as with the Guy Line Hitch. Tying ropes without slack in them is useful for many applications, like when you need to secure cargo.

Most hitches are tied by using Half Hitches in various combinations. When using more than one, Half Hitches can have a left or right orientation, and many hitches are tied by combining just two Half Hitches. Some hitches that seem different from each other are in fact made with the same exact combination of Half Hitches—the only difference may be that in one case, the hitch is tied directly onto an object, and in the other, it is tied around the standing part. An example is the difference between the Clove Hitch and the Round Turn and Two Half Hitches.

Some hitches allow you to put up to three times more strain on the rope than you are applying to tighten it. A Trucker's Hitch pulls on the rope as if you were using a pair of pulleys, allowing you to make pulling tackle from a length of rope. The magnification factor at any point is determined by how many ropes under equal tension are connected to it. Don't get confused by trying to think about which direction the rope is pulling. It helps to consider that a rope can only pull, not push.

Some hitches attach rope for pulling or hoisting large objects. The Timber Hitch is used on logs. The Barrel Sling can be used to hoist a barrel while holding it upright, and the Barrel Hitch is a sling that is tied like a Cow Hitch around an object. Its weight keeps the hitch snug.

It is rewarding to tie off a rope with the needed tension, and even be able to adjust it. Fastening ropes to objects can help with many jobs, and even more can be done when combined with other types of knots.

The more you work with hitches, the more you should have an idea of what they can do, and more importantly, what they can do for you. Fastening a rope to something is key to using rope for holding and moving objects, and it is best to learn more than one method. Also, the skills you obtain for fastening rope to objects will play an important part in how to use rope for bindings.

Barrel Hitch

If you want to lift a barrel or other short cylindrical object on its side, the Barrel Hitch can do the job of hoisting it.

Start with a strop or length of rope tied in a closed loop. Pass the end of the loop around the barrel and then through the other side of the loop. Spread the loops apart under the barrel for more stability.

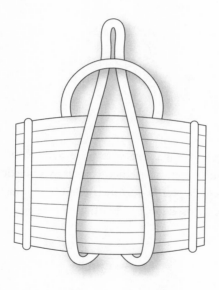

Barrel Sling

The Barrel Sling will hoist a barrel while keeping it upright.

STEP 1 Stand the barrel upright on the middle of a short length of rope, and cross the ends together on top, making an Overhand Knot around the barrel.

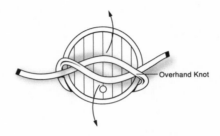

Overhand Knot

STEP 2 Spread the crossed parts of the Overhand Knot over the sides of the barrel, then tie the ends together to serve as a hoisting sling. A Fisherman's Knot (see Chapter 7) or Hunter's Bend (see Chapter 2) will work well to complete a closed loop for hoisting.

Make sure that the sling is symmetrical on the barrel before lifting.

HALF HITCH

There are two basic ways of making a Half Hitch. It can be tied off with a running end, or it can be tied off with a bight, which makes it a Slipped Half Hitch.

STEP 1 Bring the running end around the ring and then around its standing part. Then, tuck the end inside the crossing turn, next to the ring.

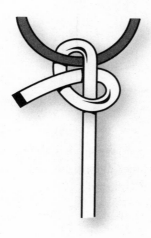

STEP 2 Another option is to make a last tuck with a bight, making it a Slipped Half Hitch.

The Half Hitch makes a very quick and temporary tie-off. It is also tied as the first step of other more secure hitches. The slipped version unties completely with just one pull.

ROLLING HITCH

The Rolling Hitch can be tied to a pole or to another rope. It provides a friction grip to resist sliding if the pull is to the side with the round turn. It works best when the pole or rope it is being tied to is twice or more the diameter of the rope used to tie the hitch.

STEP 1 Start the hitch with a round turn.

STEP 2 Cross over and finish with a Half Hitch.

STEP 3 The knot should finish with both ends coming out together under the bight.

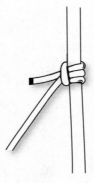

The Rolling Hitch is tied the same way as the Tautline Hitch.

Round Turn and Two Half Hitches

The instructions for tying the Round Turn and Two Half Hitches are built right into the name. It can also be thought of as tying a Clove Hitch (see Chapter 8) around its own standing part.

STEP 1   Use the running end to make a round turn over the object.

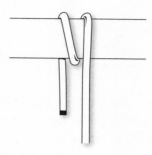

STEP 2   Tie a Half Hitch (see previous) around the standing part.

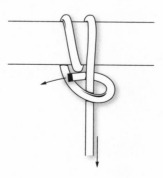

STEP 3 Next, tie a second Half Hitch.

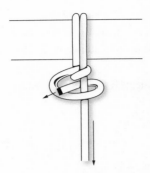

The Round Turn and Two Half Hitches is the most common hitch used for tying off a rope when you know you won't need to adjust it after tying. The most important feature of this knot is the round turn. If the rope you are tying is already under strain, the extra turn will help hold against it while making the Half Hitches and will continue to reduce the strain on the Half Hitches.

TAUTLINE HITCH

The Tautline Hitch is a very popular adjustable hitch and easy to remember if you know the Rolling Hitch (see previous). It allows you to adjust the size or tension in the rope after it is tied, making it very useful for securing cargo.

STEP 1 Bring the running end around the object to make a crossing turn, then back a distance and make two turns around the standing part.

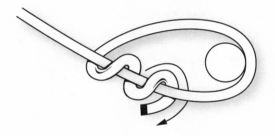

STEP 2 Finish the Rolling Hitch around the standing part.

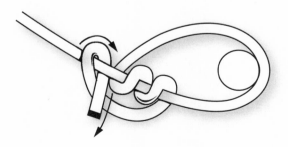

STEP 3 Tighten down the hitch.

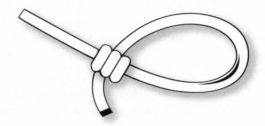

This is an easy hitch to tie, but users beware: The Tautline Hitch is not meant for heavy hoisting or for safety lines.

Trucker's Hitch

The Trucker's Hitch is tied with a Slipped Figure Eight Knot, shown in Chapter 1.

Rope bound tightly will protect cargo from shifting, but it can also damage it. Pulling a rope too tight, especially with a leveraged hitch such as the Trucker's Hitch, can crack a canoe or collapse a container. Rope can leave indentations in hardwood furniture. Use padding where the rope comes in contact with wood.

STEP 1 Start a Slipped Figure Eight Knot in the bight by making an extra twist to a crossing turn.

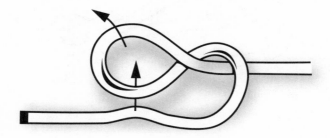

STEP 2 Finish the Slipped Figure Eight Knot by pulling a bight of the running end through it.

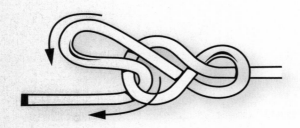

STEP 3 Treat the resulting loop as if it were a pulley by passing the running end around the anchor point and then back through the loop.

STEP 4   Bring the running end back up through the loop and pull it toward the anchor point to tighten the standing part.

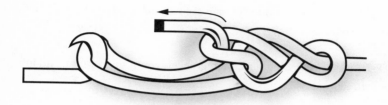

STEP 5   Secure the knot with two Half Hitches (see previous).

Make the loop as far from the anchor point as needed to take out slack in the standing part. Other loop knots can be used instead of the Slipped Figure Eight Knot, such as the Directional Figure Eight or the Butterfly Loop (see Chapter 3 for both). The Slipped Figure Eight Knot is used most often, as it is quick to tie and untie, and has a strong lead that is not very damaging to rope.

WAGONER'S HITCH

The Wagoner's Hitch is a leveraged hitch very similar to the Trucker's Hitch. It needs tension on it to stay secure, and it comes undone with just a shake.

STEP 1 Make a crossing turn, then grab a bight in the running end just below it.

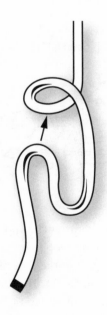

STEP 2 Pull the bight of the running end through the crossing turn. This forms a lower loop that the running end will pass through after it goes around an anchor point.

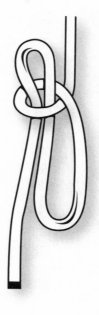

STEP 3   Pass the running end around the anchor and back up through the lower loop.

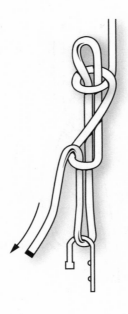

Chapter 5

SIMPLE LASHINGS

For our ancestors, a simple lashing meant the difference between swinging a sharp rock and swinging an ax. This skill remains important today, if not for axes, for lashing together poles and tying up packages and bundles.

You can use lashing bundles to secure a single object, like a box or rolled-up sleeping bag. Or you can group a stack of items, like books or newspapers. The rope or string itself can serve as a handle to lift the object. String or small cordage is often used in place of wire to bundle items in industrial applications, because wire can do more damage to any machinery it gets caught in.

Lashing two or more poles together can be very useful for both construction and repair—to give more length or to make scaffolding, ladders, or makeshift furniture. Poles can be lashed parallel to each other or at right angles.

Key to making a pole lashing is the concept of the frapping turn—that is, tight wraps of the cord around the pole. While the multiple wraps around two poles provide the structural strength that a lashing needs, the frapping constricts the wraps and creates the tension that holds them in place. If the poles are tied together parallel to each other as in the

Sheer Lashing, the wraps must be loose enough to allow a couple of frapping turns to pass between them.

If you're attempting to lash poles that are not exactly parallel or at right angles to one another, position them parallel and loosely tie a Sheer Lashing. The lashing will tighten as the poles are twisted open. You can do this with three poles to make a tripod.

Diagonal Lashing

Whereas Square Lashing would be used to attach poles at right angles, the Diagonal Lashing is used to keep two crossed poles rigid with respect to each other. Scaffoldings made with a combination of these two lashings are very rigid and secure.

STEP 1 Cross two poles diagonally, and make a Timber Hitch (see Chapter 10) around them.

STEP 2 Pull the Timber Hitch tight and make three vertical wraps around the center.

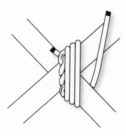

STEP 3   Cross over and make three more wraps around the opposite diagonal.

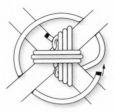

STEP 4   Make two frapping turns, below the upper pole and above the lower pole, just as with the Sheer Lashing. Finish with a Clove Hitch (see Chapter 8).

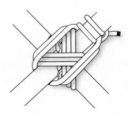

Sheer Lashing

Also called Round Lashing, this method will bind two poles parallel to each other.

STEP 1 Anchor the rope to one of the poles with a Clove Hitch (see Chapter 8).

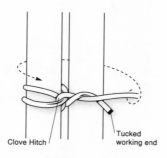

Clove Hitch

Tucked working end

STEP 2 Wrap the rope around both poles with light and even tension, leaving enough space between them for the frapping turns. Continue making wraps until you cover a distance that's about twice the width of a single pole.

STEP 3   Make two frapping turns and finish with a Clove Hitch.

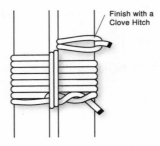

Finish with a
Clove Hitch

STEP 4   If the lashing is not too tight, the legs can be spread to use as "sheer" poles.

←— Splay legs —→

If the poles need to be spread to make an A-frame, make sure the tension is moderate. If they need to stay very rigid with each other, try using more than one Sheer Lashing. Three poles can be tied in similar fashion, with frapping turns between each pair of poles.

Square Lashing

If you are making scaffolding or other large square frames, Square Lashing is the method to use on the corners that meet at right angles.

STEP 1 Arrange two poles at a 90-degree angle to each other. Anchor one end with a Clove Hitch (see Chapter 8) and start wraps, as shown.

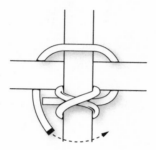

STEP 2 Make four wraps, passing over the pole at the top, and under the pole at the bottom, keeping each wrap tight.

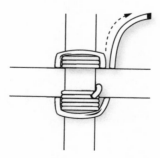

STEP 3 Make two frapping turns, staying in front of the back pole and behind the front pole, just as you would do with a Sheer Lashing.

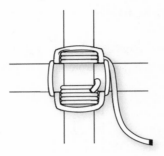

STEP 4 Tie off the remaining end with a Clove Hitch.

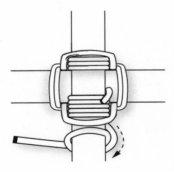

Note that no slack needs to be saved for the frapping turns, so keep tension on at all stages of this knot.

Transom Knot

The Transom Knot is a good way to tie two sticks perpendicular to each other if you want a lashing that is not bulky. The ends can be cut off close to the knot.

STEP 1 Arrange the two sticks so that one is laid across the length of the other, and tie them together with a Double Overhand Noose Knot (see Chapter 10).

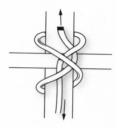

STEP 2 Tighten the rope by pulling the ends in opposite directions.

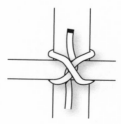

The top part of this knot has the same crossings as the Constrictor Knot, which is why this simple little knot grabs so well.

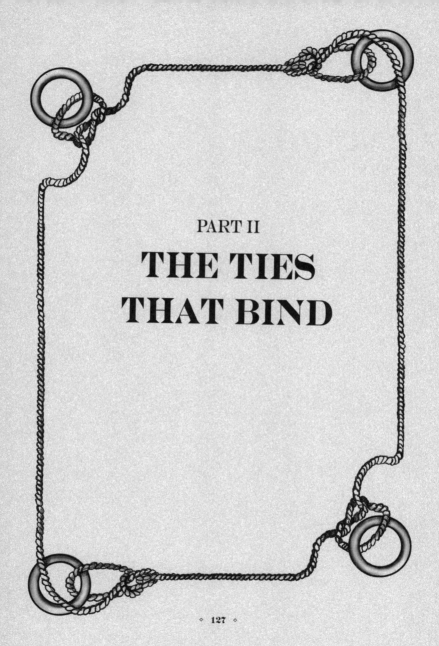

PART II

THE TIES THAT BIND

Chapter 6

NAUTICAL KNOTS

Different knots have different properties that make them useful for specific tasks. Some knots are especially secure, while others are good for quick release. Some are useful because they can be easily adjusted, while others are preferred because they stay locked. Even the appearance of a finished knot can be important, whether to confirm that it has been tied correctly or for decoration.

Knots are an integral part of the sport and business of sailing—so much so that many knots were first invented by sailors. In the days of clippers and square-riggers, when the upper deck of a vessel was a maze of ropes and cords, choosing and tying the correct knot—one that could be relied upon to do its job—could literally mean the difference between life and death.

On shipboard, knots and ropes still control such essential things as sails, mooring, docking, anchoring, and ensuring that cargo will not shift during the voyage. Knots were also used by sailors to mark their speed—essential in the days when navigation was a less scientifically exact procedure than today. The pilot or navigator would tie a cord to a piece of wood, weighted so that it would float upright in the water and resist the speed of the waves and of the vessel itself. Knots were tied in the cord at a distance of 47 feet 3 inches from one another. The wood (or "chip") was tossed overboard and, as one sailor counted the time, another played out the cord. The ship's speed was thus calculated in "knots"—a knot is approximately 1.85 kilometers per hour.

Sailors were also responsible for the spread of knots and knotting techniques around the world, since their travels took them to all corners of the globe. The knots you will find in the following pages are only a small sampling of the infinite variety of knots we owe to the travels of seafolk.

ANCHOR HITCH

Also called the Fisherman's Bend, even though it is a hitch and not a bend, the Anchor Hitch is commonly used to tie a rope to an anchor.

STEP 1   Start with a round turn and pass a Half Hitch (see Chapter 4) through both turns.

STEP 2   Finish with a regular Half Hitch.

The Anchor Hitch stays secure when the rope drifts and the strength of pull changes. For larger boats, this hitch is relied on for repair more than a permanent connection. You can make the Anchor Hitch more secure by seizing the running end to the standing part (see Appendix A for information on seizing).

BOWLINE IN THE BIGHT

This knot is similar to the regular Bowline, except that you start out by folding the end of the rope into a bight.

STEP 1   Make a crossing turn and bring the end up through it.

STEP 2   Open up the end loop and bring it down and under the two loops.

STEP 3 Bring the end loop up behind the standing parts and tighten down.

The Bowline in the Bight is quick, fun to tie, and makes a nice double loop. If tied near the end of a rope, the running end can be secured to the standing part with yet another Bowline. Just make a crossing turn in the standing part and bring the running end up through it, around the standing part, and back down through the crossing turn just like in a Bowline. This can be done with any knot where the running end comes out of the knot parallel to the standing part.

BUNTLINE HITCH

The name of the Buntline Hitch comes from its use on sailing ships as a hitch that would not shake free when both the rope and the sail (a bunt is the middle portion of a sail) it was tied to moved in the wind.

Make one turn around the object, then make two Half Hitches (as shown). Note that the second Half Hitch is between the object and the first Half Hitch.

This hitch traps the running end very tightly. Learn this knot, and you will also know how to tie a common necktie knot.

Cleat Hitch

When tied correctly, the Cleat Hitch has a distinctive loop, with one line on top crossing two parallel lines under it.

STEP 1   Pass the line once around the base, and bring it diagonally across the top.

STEP 2   Pass the running end under one end of the cleat and back diagonally across and on top of the previous pass.

STEP 3 Form a crossing turn with the running end on the bottom.

STEP 4 Next, drop the crossing turn over the cleat end and pull tight.

STEP 5 Or you could finish with a quick-release slipped version.

The most common mistake with this hitch is to make too many wraps and crossings, which can cause it to jam when releasing, making you look like you don't belong near a boat. The Cleat Hitch is not considered a permanent connection but is fairly secure when the rope used is not too big or small for the horn cleat. The slipped version needs a steady load to keep its hold.

CONSTRICTOR KNOT

Start this knot exactly as you would the Clove Hitch (see Chapter 8). Only the last tuck is different, as shown in Step 3.

STEP 1 Pass the running end over and around the pole, crossing over the standing part, and behind the pole.

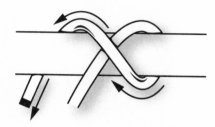

STEP 2 Bring the running end from behind the pole and up over the standing part.

STEP 3   Tuck the end under the center X-shaped part of the knot. If you are able to place the Constrictor Knot at the end of the pole or another object, you can use the following method.

STEP 4   Make a single turn around the end of the pole, then pull down on the bottom part of the turn and twist it to make a crossing turn.

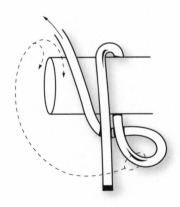

STEP 5   Pull the crossing turn over the standing part and the end of the pole.

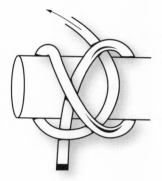

This knot earns its name well, constricting tighter as the ends are pulled in opposite directions. This is a very popular knot because it functions much like a hose clamp. For best results, use soft cord for binding a hard object, and hard cord for binding a soft object. It is difficult to untie, but completely releases when the topmost crossing is cut. The last tuck can also be made with a bight to make a much more easily released slipped version.

EYE SPLICE

Before you begin, you need to splice the running end. Unlay several inches of a three-strand rope, and tape or bind the area to keep the rope from unlaying further. The tucks start in a staggered order and proceed in an over-and-under pattern, just as when tying the Back Splice (see Chapter 1).

STEP 1   Make the first tuck by inserting the first unlaid strand through the intact strands of the rope.

STEP 2   Start the next tuck by inserting the next unlaid strand through the same intact section of the rope, but this time tucking over and under.

STEP 3   Turn over the rope, and start the third tuck under the remaining strand.

STEP 4   Continue tucks in an over-and-under pattern.

An Eye Splice is used to make a permanent loop in three-strand rope. It retains all of the strength of the rope, making it stronger than a regular loop knot. It is sometimes tied tightly around a protective thimble to protect the inside of the loop from abrasion. Each strand is usually tucked three times for natural fiber ropes, and up to five is sometimes used for more slippery synthetics. Sometimes the strands are thinned out after each level of tucks to taper the splice.

HEAVING LINE KNOT

The Heaving Line Knot, also known as the Monk's Knot, gets its name from the heaving line—a smaller line made to heave from a boat to dock so that it can be used to pull a heavier line over.

STEP 1   Double the line back for the length desired, and then begin tightly wrapping the running end around the doubled-up rope, making concentric circles to the left.

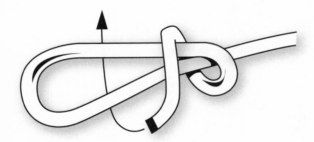

STEP 2   As you get to the end, tuck the running end through the last of the remaining bight. Pulling on the standing part will tighten this last tuck in place.

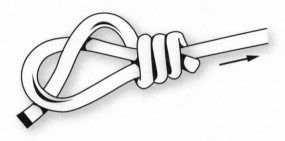

The Heaving Line Knot is useful for shortening a line and for weighting the end for heaving, if necessary. It is also used decoratively.

MARLINESPIKE HITCH

The Marlinespike Hitch is named after a small metal bar used as a tying tool. It is tapered to a point at one end, which can be inserted into knots to work them loose, or into the strands of rope to aid with splicing.

STEP 1 Twist the tip of the marlinespike so that the rope forms a crossing turn over it.

STEP 2 Pull the bight across the standing part, forming what looks like an Overhand Knot.

STEP 3 Lift the bight of the standing part up through the crossing turn.

With the use of a Marlinespike Hitch, string or other small cordage can quickly and easily be attached to the marlinespike. By holding the marlinespike in your fist with the standing part of the hitch coming out between your two middle fingers, you can pull forcefully without the string cutting into your hand. A lashing or seizing can be made very tight this way.

Oysterman's Stopper

The Oysterman's Stopper Knot begins by tying the Slipped Noose (see Chapter 10).

STEP 1 Tie a Slipped Noose, making a tuck through the loop.

STEP 2 Tuck the running end through the noose.

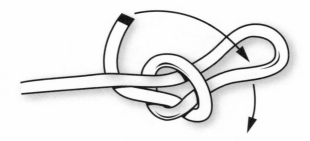

STEP 3 Pull the standing part to trap the running end with the loop.

STEP 4 As you tighten the knot, you should get the finished Oyster-man's Stopper.

When tightened down, the face of this knot has a unique trefoil appearance. This knot is wider than the overhand stopper knots. An alternative way to tie this knot is to make a Bowline Loop (see Chapter 3), made so small that it is right up against the knot. It will be facing the wrong way, but can be reversed if, while there is still a bit of slack, the center is pulled through the middle by bracing the knot and pulling on the running end. This reversal is called "capsizing."

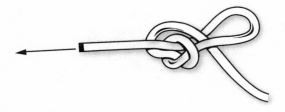

REEF KNOT

Also called the Square Knot, this knot has been in common use for centuries for tying packages and bundles of all kinds (not to mention shoe laces). It is also used to tie bandages because it lies flat, making the dressing more effective and comfortable.

It should be said that the Reef Knot is notorious for easily coming undone, to the point that it is used in magic tricks to give the appearance of "magically" untying two ropes without effort. It is especially unstable if the ropes used are of different sizes of materials.

STEP 1 Pass one end over and around the other, making a Half Knot, just as if you were tying an Overhand Knot with two ends of the same piece.

First Working End

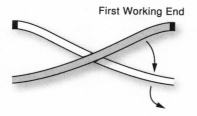

STEP 2 Tie a second Half Knot by tucking the right end over the left one.

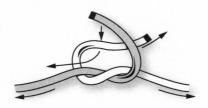

STEP 3 Pull on both ends to tighten. Note that each end will exit next to its standing part.

Finished knot is symmetrical

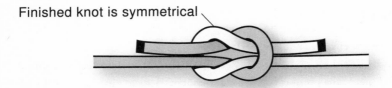

As you tie the Reef Knot, it may help you to say to yourself, "Left over right, right over left." To loosen the knot quickly, jerk one of the ends over the knot away from its own standing end, causing the knot to capsize. There are two common mistakes made with this knot. One is to make both Half Knots the same, making a very poor Granny Knot, and the other is to use this knot as a bend, which is not reliable.

RUNNING BOWLINE

You can tie a Running Bowline by tying a Bowline (see Chapter 3) around its own standing part or by tying a Bowline the usual way, and then pulling a bight of the standing part through the loop.

STEP 1 Tie the Running Bowline by tying a Bowline around the standing part.

STEP 2 The result: Running Bowline.

If you make a fixed-loop knot like the Bowline or any other fixed-loop knot, and decide the loop part is not big enough, just turn it into a running loop knot and have the loop as big as you need it. Because the fixed-loop part does not lock onto or grip the standing part, the noose will slide open easily even if great tension is placed on the sliding loop.

Chapter 7

FISHING KNOTS

The history of fishing has been the history of a continuous evolution and improvement of lines and the knots tied in those lines. Fishing dates back to at least the Paleolithic period; hooks have been found from the Stone Age, so our ancestors clearly had some form of cord and a method of tying the hooks into it. (Fishermen also used various types of spears, which is possibly one reason why Neptune, the Roman god of the sea, is depicted holding a trident.) Ancient fishing lines were made from shredded papyrus leaves, leather, or animal hair, and must have been clumsy and difficult to knot properly.

In the fifteenth century an English abbess, Juliana Berners, wrote a book, *A Treatyse of Fysshynge wyth an Angle,* which included some advice about tying knots. (Lest you think it weird that the head of a religious establishment would write a book about fishing, remember that convents and monasteries depended on fish for a good deal of their food.) Back then, fishing lines were largely made of braided horsehair, which was clumsy and often broke.

Since then, fishermen have refined their lines to be thinner and stronger and their knots, whether for rod-and-reel fishing or net fishing, to be sturdier and more effective. The invention of nylon in the 1930s initiated the modern era of fishing.

For the enthusiastic pliers of the art and craft of fishing, here is a selection of popular knots.

ANGLER'S LOOP

Both strong and secure, the Angler's Loop is a great general-purpose knot. Because it is difficult to untie, this knot is meant to be permanent, usually tied in small cordage or fishing line. When tightened down evenly, it makes an excellent knot to use with bungee cord.

STEP 1 Form an Overhand Knot, and tuck the running end back through it.

STEP 2 Trace the running end behind and around the standing part, and back through the knot.

STEP 3 Tighten down the knot by pulling on all leads.

To tie the knot more quickly, note that tying a slipknot is a quick way to finish the first step.

DOUBLE UNI-KNOT

Whereas the Fisherman's Knot and Double Fisherman's Knot make a bend by tying an Overhand Knot around each other's standing part, this excellent bend, called the Double Uni-Knot or the Double Grinner Knot, uses four or more Overhand Knots. The Double Uni-Knot is great for joining fishing lines.

STEP 1 Overlap the ends of two ropes and use one end to tie a multiple Overhand Knot around the standing part of the other line.

STEP 2 Tighten down, as shown.

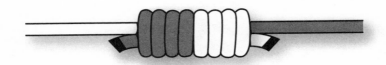

DROPPER LOOP

Also called the Blood Loop, the Dropper Loop is yet another useful fishing knot based on the series of Overhand Knots.

STEP 1   Make a Multiple Overhand Knot with four tucks.

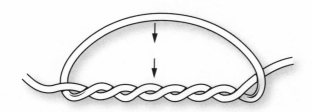

STEP 2   Pull the center of the bight or belly through the center part of the spine.

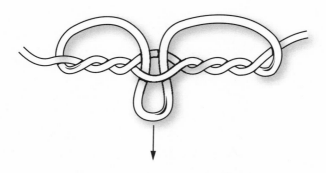

STEP 3 Tighten the loop.

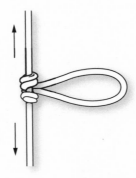

The Dropper Loop can be used to position additional flies, weights, or hooks along a fishing line.

FISHERMAN'S KNOT

Even though this is really a bend, it is known as the Fisherman's Knot, Englishman's Knot, and the Angler's Knot.

STEP 1 Lay two ropes parallel to each other and overlap each rope's running end around the other's standing part, making two Overhand Knots.

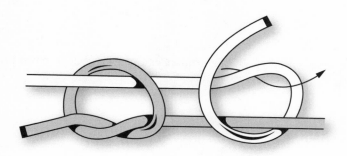

STEP 2 Tighten each Overhand by pulling on the two standing parts, so that the two ropes are held firmly together.

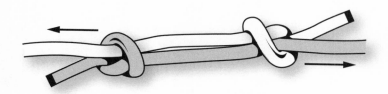

STEP 3 Pull the two ropes apart so that they form a circle, tightening each knot.

The Fisherman's Knot is difficult to untie and will work best when tied in small cordage. It is often chosen as a secure way to join two small lines of similar size.

Double Fisherman's Knot

The Double Fisherman's Knot is a bend tied in the same manner as the Fisherman's Knot, with two Double Overhand Knots in place of the regular ones.

STEP 1 Lay two ropes parallel to each other and tie a Double Overhand Knot (see Chapter 1) on each of the two sides.

STEP 2 Tighten up each Double Overhand Knot and pull the two ropes apart so that they form a circle, further tightening the knots.

This bend provides more security than the Fisherman's Knot, which you may need if you use very slippery lines or they differ in size a bit. If you need more security than that, you may consider using Triple Overhand Knots (see Chapter 1) to fasten the two ropes. If more than a Triple is to be used in fishing line, it should be tied in the same manner as the Uni-Knot (see further).

IMPROVED CLINCH KNOT

This knot is a useful fishing knot that works well with thin monofilament.

STEP 1 Pass the running end through the hook eye or other attachment point, then make three to five wraps around the standing part.

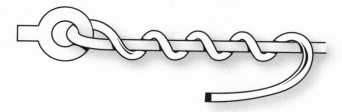

STEP 2 Bring the running end back and thread it through the crossing turn closest to the eye.

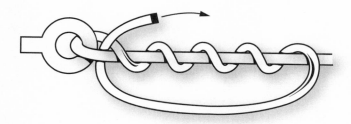

STEP 3 Tuck the running end through its own bight. Tighten by pulling on the standing part. If there's slack, pull the running end.

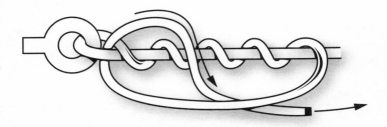

Thin monofilament requires more wraps than thicker line does, and even one wrap can make the difference as to whether it slips under strain. It is difficult to pull this knot down when tied in thick line.

LOBSTER BUOY HITCH

The Lobster Buoy Hitch is tied with just one turn around the object because using a round turn would take tension away from Half Hitches, reducing the advantage of trapping the running end.

Bring the running end once around the object. Make two Half Hitches that form a Cow Hitch (see Chapter 11) around the standing part, so that the running end is trapped against the object.

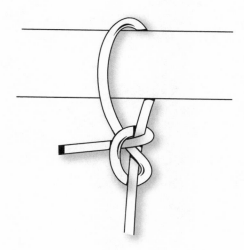

A useful feature of this hitch is that the running end is trapped, but not as tightly as in the Buntline Hitch.

Palomar Hook Knot

Because the Palomar Hook Knot is strong and secure, many recreational and professional fishermen make it their favorite hook tie.

STEP 1 Fold the end of the line over and pull the bight through the eye of hook or lure.

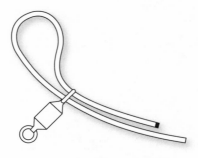

STEP 2 Use the bight to tie an Overhand Knot.

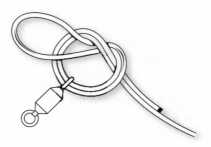

STEP 3 Pass the hook or swivel through the bight of the running end. Take out slack with both ends together, and finish tightening with the standing part.

Note that in order to tie the Palomar, the eye should be large enough to pass a bight through it.

REEL KNOT

Also called the Arbor Knot or Line to Reel or Spool, this knot will get you started when winding line onto a spool.

STEP 1 Bring the running end around the spool and tie an Overhand Knot around the standing part.

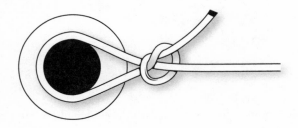

STEP 2 Make another Overhand Knot, close to the first, and trim the end short.

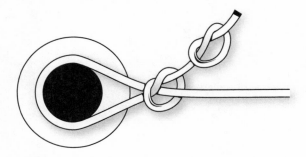

The second Overhand Knot should be tied close to the first, and the very tip should be cut short to avoid tangling with the line as it is wound to the spool. Fingernail clippers make easy work of cutting fishing line close to a knot, but take care not to nick the knot with the clippers.

UNI-KNOT

Also called the Grinner Knot, the Uni-Knot makes for a strong attachment to hooks, lures, or swivels.

STEP 1   Pass the running end through the eye, bring it back along the standing part, and form a Multiple Overhand Knot.

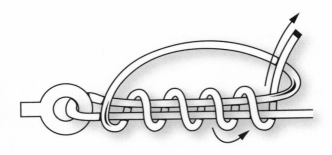

STEP 2   Tighten so that the bight makes wraps around the center.

The Multiple Overhand Knot can be tightened down on the standing part, without closing it down to the object to make a loop knot, allowing an attached lure to move more freely and realistically in the water.

Chapter 8

CLIMBING KNOTS

In May 2012, a British mountaineer was practicing his techniques on a climbing wall in Gloucestershire. He attempted to tie a bowline, his usual knot, but either failed to do so or did so improperly. The knot failed, and he fell thirty feet to his death.

That such an accident could happen in the controlled environment of a climbing wall was unusual. Sadly, it is more frequent when climbers are in the open, particularly in extreme conditions of high altitude and freezing cold. In such places, a climber's life lies in her or his mastery of the craft of the knot. Experienced climbers learn to double- and triple-check their knots and to make sure the knot will do precisely what it is supposed to do.

One reason climbers often choose certain kinds of knots is that it is easy to tell at a glance if they've been tied correctly. Nonetheless, it must be stressed that climbing is a sport in which climbers rely upon one another, and thus they must be able to trust that their fellow climbers are expert knot tyers.

Here are some of the more commonly used climbing knots.

CLOVE HITCH

This hitch ties quickly, but should not be considered a permanent connection or be used for safety or heavy loads.

STEP 1 Pass the running end around the object, cross over the standing part, and then pass the running end around the object again; then tuck it under the last crossing.

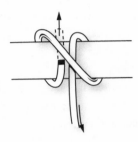

STEP 2 Tighten the knot around the object. Because the Clove Hitch can be tied in the bight, you can use any section of the rope to make the hitch that slides over posts.

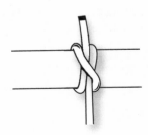

STEP 3 Make two crossing turns and pass one in front of the other.

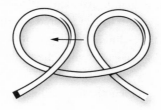

STEP 4 Place the formed double loop around the object to form the Clove Hitch.

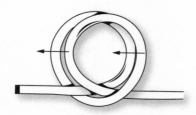

The Clove Hitch Knot is also the basis for other knots, and the last tuck can be slipped if a quick release is desired.

ICICLE HITCH

John Smith of Surrey, England, first demonstrated the Icicle Hitch by using it to suspend his weight from a tapered wooden fid that was hanging point-down from the ceiling. Like finger cuffs, this hitch will shrink to grab strongly, then loosen easily when the strain is taken off.

STEP 1 Start with a good length of running end and make a crossing shown here.

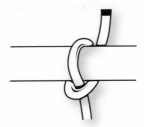

STEP 2 Cross the running end to the left and behind the pole.

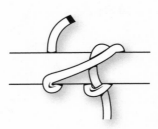

STEP 3 Bring the running end around the pole, tucking it under the crossing. Complete four turns, tucking the end each time.

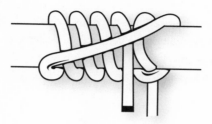

STEP 4 After the fourth turn, also tuck the running end under the first loop so that both ends exit together.

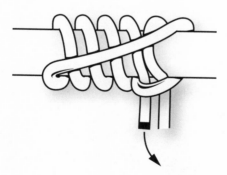

After you are finished, use the running end as the end that will take strain. This will allow the hitch to have its tenacious grip. Do this either by leaving a large excess of running end or by extending it by making a bend to another rope.

You can also tie the Icicle Hitch near the end of a pole, in a manner similar to the Pile Hitch (See Chapter 10). To see this, first tie it near a pole end with the method shown previously, then pull the bight over the end as if you were untying the Pile Hitch, and you will see the setup for this method. When checking to see if you have tied it correctly, keep in mind that this hitch is basically an extended Pile Hitch.

PORTUGUESE BOWLINE

Before you start practicing this knot, review the steps for tying the regular Bowline Loop (see Chapter 3). Once you learn the Bowline, this knot is quick and easy to remember.

STEP 1   Start as you would to tie a regular Bowline, then use the running end to make a second loop.

STEP 2   Continue the same as you would with a Bowline.

STEP 3 Finish by making the final tuck.

With the Portuguese Bowline, you'll have two loops that can be adjusted in relative size after the loop is tied, but the strain on both must be equal.

Triple Bowline

Another version of the Bowline Loop (see Chapter 3) that is tied using a doubled-up rope.

STEP 1 Starting with a bight, tie the doubled-up rope just as you would the Bowline.

STEP 2 Finish by tightening.

This loop knot is also good for fastening to multiple anchor points. It is easy to remember, and with a little practice you can make each of the loops different sizes.

Chapter 9

PACKING KNOTS

During the holiday season, it's possible you've found yourself struggling to tie recalcitrant bits of ribbon or string, all the while muttering things under your breath that run quite contrary to the season's festive mood. That's quite unnecessary, because there are plenty of knots that can be used to secure packages, whether for shipping them through the mail or handing them to someone yourself.

The most important thing about packing knots is that they be secure and not slip, no matter how much handling they receive. Some of these knots will be familiar to you (the Granny Knot is among the most commonly used of all knots), while others will not. With a little practice, you can learn to tie packages in a strong, secure, and even decorative way that will be the envy of all your friends.

Butcher's Knot

Back when most people got their meat from a neighborhood butcher, the Butcher's Knot was commonly used to secure joints of meat. Nowadays, when meat usually comes in sterilized plastic packages on the supermarket shelf, it has become a bit less common, but you can still find it in use at butcher shops.

STEP 1   Tie a Figure Eight Knot (see Chapter 1) near the running end. Then, pass the standing part over and around the object, so that it comes back out through the bottom of the Figure Eight.

STEP 2   Make a Half Hitch (see Chapter 4) with the standing part around the running end of the Figure Eight.

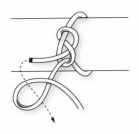

STEP 3 Finish the knot by tightening.

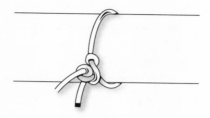

As you tighten the knot, hold tension on the running end of the Figure Eight Knot. This will aid in holding the wrap tight while making the final Half Hitch. The Butcher's Knot should not be considered a permanent binding, but you can make it more secure by adding an Overhand Knot to the running end of the Figure Eight Knot.

Chainstitch Lashing

Chainstitch Lashing holds well on bundles that are awkwardly shaped or that flex. You can also use it for decorative purposes.

STEP 1 Make a Timber Hitch (see Chapter 10) at one end of the bundle. Fold a bight in the running end close to the Timber Hitch and then pull another bight through it after first passing it around the bundle.

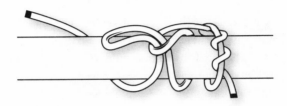

STEP 2 Continue passing new bights around and through the previous bight. To finish, pull the entire running end through the last bight (instead of another bight) and secure with two Half Hitches (see Chapter 4).

Though it may look complicated, Chainstitch Lashing ties quickly once you get the knack.

GRANNY KNOT

The Granny Knot is a variation on the Reef Knot (see Chapter 6), except that the two Half Knots are the same.

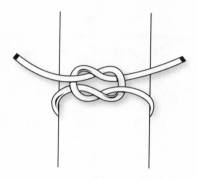

Also called the Garden Knot, the Granny Knot is tied often just because it is what you get when you make both crossings for the Half Knots with either hand. You will likely see it tied by store clerks in the handles of plastic shopping bags. This knot will either slip or jam, and can be difficult to untie. People often tie the double slipped version of this knot when attempting to tie a Double Slipped Reef in their shoelaces, which is evident when the knot's bows run up and down the length of the shoe instead of across.

MARLING

This type of lashing relies on Marling Hitches to hold the contents of a bundle firmly in place.

STEP 1   Start by securing the rope around the end of the bundle with a Timber Hitch (see Chapter 10). Lead the running end partway down the bundle, make another wrap, and tuck the running end over and under, as shown.

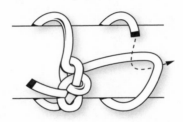

STEP 2   Continue with a few additional wraps along the length of the bundle. To secure the last Marling Hitch, tie one or two Half Hitches (see Chapter 4).

Parcel Tie

The Parcel Tie is a good method of tying a package or a stack of books or newspapers.

STEP 1 Tie a Bowline Loop (see Chapter 3) at the end of a length of rope.

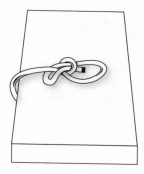

STEP 2 Pass the rope around the package and through the loop, then lead it around the package again, but at a right angle to the first crossing.

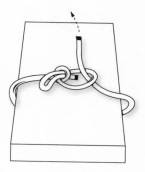

STEP 3 As you cross the length of rope with the running end underneath the package, maneuver it to tie a Crossing Knot (the illustration here is the view of the underside).

STEP 4 Next, bring the running end around to the front and pass it through the loop again.

STEP 5 Finish by securing the end with two Half Hitches (see Chapter 4).

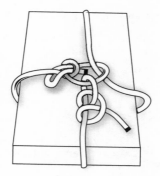

Thanks to the properties of the Crossing Knot (a knot made by one rope around another at the point where it crosses it, then continuing past it), you should have no problem lifting up the bundle by pulling on the knotted rope.

Slipped and Double Slipped Reef Knots

Here are two other variations on tying a Reef Knot.

STEP 1 To make a Slipped Reef Knot, start by tying the Reef Knot (see Chapter 6), but tuck one of the ends with a bight.

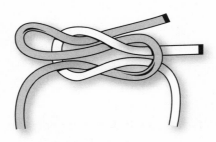

STEP 2 To make a Double Slipped Reef Knot, tie the second Half Knot with bights at both ends.

The Reef Knot is commonly slipped for ease of untying or for decoration. The Double Slipped Reef is commonly used to tie shoes and is tied with ribbon around packages to accentuate the decorative bows.

STEVEDORE KNOT

This knot begins like the Overhand, but here the running end makes two complete round turns around the standing part before passing through its loop.

Make a crossing turn with the running end by passing it down, over the standing part, down behind it, up over it, down behind it again, and through the loop. Pull on the standing part and running end to tighten.

The name of this knot refers to the profession of dockworkers, who were said to use this as a stopper knot. Although it is not wider than the Figure Eight, it is bulkier and has a distinctive look when pulled down as a stopper knot. This knot is difficult to pull down to stopper knot form when tied by twisting the crossing turn.

Chapter 10

HOUSEHOLD KNOTS

Whether it's tying a knot to truss a chicken for dinner, hanging a clothes-line, or hanging a child's swing, knots are an everyday occurrence around any household. For the most part, we barely give them any thought.

Yet, with a little practice and care, we can tie knots that will do the job right and won't cause us frustration or concern by giving way at awkward moments. You may even find some new uses for them that you hadn't anticipated.

BOA CONSTRICTOR

Also known as the Boa Knot, the Boa Constrictor forms an even more tenacious hold than the regular Constrictor Knot.

STEP 1 Begin by forming two crossing turns.

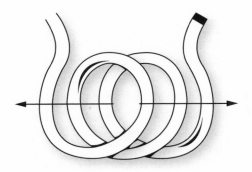

STEP 2 Overlap the crossing turns and twist one end over by a half turn.

STEP 3 Place over the end of a pole, as shown. (The ends can be folded up to ease placement.)

STEP 4 Tighten by pulling the ends in opposite directions.

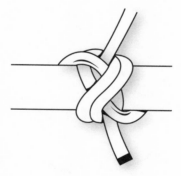

To learn how to tie this knot around a bar without access to an end, first tie it with this method, place it over a bar or pole end, then untie with just one end to see how the wraps and tucks are made.

DOUBLE OVERHAND NOOSE

Also called the Poacher's Noose, the Poacher's Knot, and the Strangle Snare, this knot is a very good general-purpose noose to learn.

STEP 1 Tie a Double Overhand Knot (see Chapter 1) with the running end over the standing part.

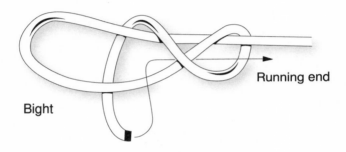

Running end

Bight

STEP 2 Tighten as shown.

Noose

Standing part

Because the Double Overhand Knot can hold tension when tightened down, the loop opening will not close down until it is pulled on, which helps to explain its nefarious past with poachers. Knots that make use of the Double Overhand structure remain very useful today due to their high security even when tied with slippery synthetic cordage. The Triple Overhand version of this knot is even more secure.

GUY LINE HITCH

A "guy line" is a rope or wire used to hold a pole, antenna mast, or tent in place. There is generally more than one guy line, and when the Guy Line Hitch is used, the length and tension of each can quickly be adjusted.

STEP 1 Make an Overhand Knot some distance from the end, so that you leave enough running end to pass around the object and then back to the Overhand.

STEP 2 Pass the running end back through the bottom of the Overhand Knot.

Sometimes two Overhand Knots are tied next to each other in the standing part. The running end is passed through the first one to provide the grip and the second one to hold the end down.

Tie two Overhand Knots in the standing part, and tuck the running end into the second one.

Like the Tautline Hitch, the Guy Line Hitch is meant for a support line and not for serious hoisting or for rescue and safety lines.

Hangman's Noose

This noose is also called Jack Ketch's Knot, named after a well-known hangman. It handles shock loads, and is also a handy way to store rope.

Never toy with the Hangman's Noose, and be particularly careful with it around children. Nooses can also be highly offensive in some situations and should *only* be used where there is a specific reason for them.

STEP 1 Fold the running end back along the standing part, and fold the new running end back on itself. Wrap the running end around the standing part, moving from bottom to top.

STEP 2   Tuck the running end through the top bight.

STEP 3   Put tension on the knot by pulling on the bottom loop.

HONDA KNOT

Also called the Lariat Knot and the Bowstring Knot, this knot can be used to make an especially small loop because it is circular instead of oval, like most loops.

STEP 1   Tie an Overhand Knot, then lead the running end back through it, finishing with another Overhand Knot at the tip. Then tighten down the first Overhand Knot. The second Overhand locks the loop.

STEP 2   If a running loop is desired, the Honda Knot itself can be tied around its standing part.

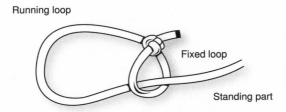

Running loop

Fixed loop

Standing part

As you pass the running end through the Overhand Knot in Step 1, it helps to remember that Overhand Knots have three openings. To be tied correctly, you must lead the running end through the opening closest to the loop, and take care that it stays in this part when tightening. If the lead slips into the middle part, the knot will not be secure.

The Honda Knot makes a good low-friction running loop. It is used to make a lariat, which is a running loop also known as a lasso. This knot has been used to tie off bowstrings because the size of the loop can be adjusted by changing the place of the Overhand Knot on the tip.

It's worth noting that the Honda Knot is tied in the same manner as the Guy Line Hitch. It is how they are used that makes them different. The Honda Knot is used when a locking loop is desired, and the Guy Line Hitch is used when the size of the loop will need to be decreased one or more times, thereby shortening the line it is tying off. If needed, however, the Honda Knot can be adjusted in size by changing the place on the locking Overhand Knot. This adjustability is why the Honda Knot has been used to attach bowstrings.

PILE HITCH

The Pile Hitch is very quick and easy to tie, as long as you're working at the end of a stick or pole.

STEP 1 Pass a bight of rope around a post near the edge.

STEP 2 Open up the bight to pass it over the two standing parts and through the top of the post.

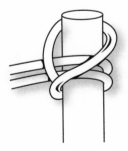

It helps to learn tying the Pile Hitch before going on to the Icicle Hitch (see Chapter 8), which is an extension of the Pile Hitch.

SLIPPED OVERHAND KNOT

You start the Slipped Overhand Knot the same way you begin tying the Overhand Knot, with one variation—the last tuck is made with a bight of the running end, so that the very end is not pulled through the crossing turn. This is what you do when you tie the bows in your shoelaces.

Pass the running end around the standing part, making a loop; then, make a bight in the running end and pass it through the crossing turn. Pull on the standing part and the bight to tighten.

Whereas the Overhand Knot can be difficult to untie, this knot can be untied simply by pulling on the running end to take out the last tuck, just as you do when you untie shoelaces. However, this trick does not work with all knots, as not all knots can be released by letting out the last tuck.

Slipped Noose

This knot is similar to the Slipped Overhand Knot. The difference is that the last tuck is made with a bight of the standing part, instead of the running end.

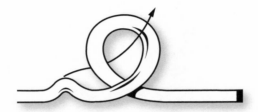

Pass the running end around the standing part, making a loop; then, make a bight in the standing part and pass it through the crossing turn. Pull on the running end and on the bight loop to tighten.

It is important to learn the difference between the Slipped Overhand Knot and the Slipped Noose. Each one will serve you as the starting point for other knots.

Surgeon's Knot

Used by surgeons to tie off blood vessels, the Surgeon's Knot works well with small and slippery tying materials. Because the first crossing is double, it holds tension better than a Half Knot while completing the top half of the knot.

STEP 1 Make the bottom half of the knot with two crossings instead of the single crossing of the Half Knot.

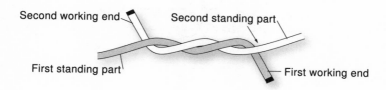

Second working end · Second standing part · First standing part · First working end

STEP 2 Finish the top half with a single crossing, as for the Reef Knot (see Chapter 6).

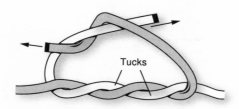

Tucks

If you wish, you can also tie the top half of the Surgeon's Knot with two crossings.

Timber Hitch

Just as its name suggests, the Timber Hitch is traditionally used to hoist or drag logs or poles.

STEP 1   Start by tying a Half Hitch (see Chapter 4).

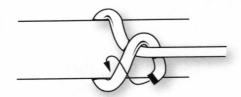

STEP 2   Continue making additional wraps, as shown.

As you can see, this hitch will work best if you place strain on it along the direction of the object the rope is hitched to—it will keep the knot tight.

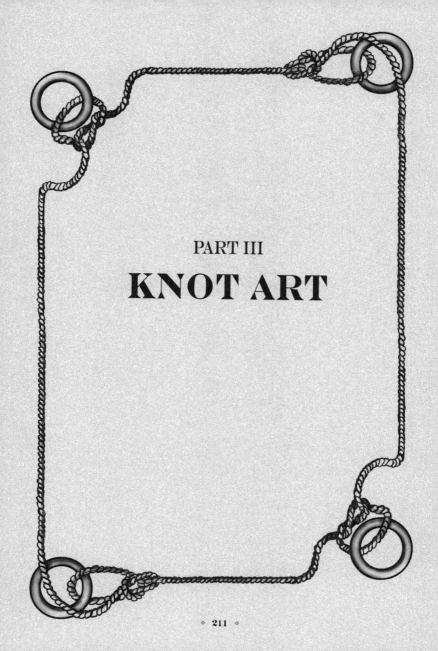

PART III

KNOT ART

Chapter 11

DECORATIVE KNOTTING

As remarked in the introduction, knots have been with us practically as long as there have been humans to tie them. Among their earliest uses (in addition to securing things) were recordkeeping and measurement. But they were also used extensively for decorative purposes.

In Western society, knots often appeared in heraldry, as particular knots became associated with various family trees. In the East, some decorative knots were held to have mystic symbolism or to bring good luck. (Western traditions have occasionally connected knots with luck as well; when Alexander cut the Gordian Knot, an oracle predicted that he would become king of Asia, a prophecy that was fulfilled, if only for a short time.)

Entire art forms (for example, macramé) have been developed using knots. It could also be said that knitting and crocheting are essentially based on creating knots.

Here, for your interest, are some of the more common decorative knots.

Cow Hitch

Also called the Lark's Head, the Cow Hitch is used in decorative work. It is only considered secure if the tension is on both ends.

STEP 1 Start by making a double crossing turn over an object.

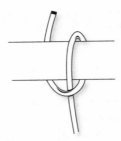

STEP 2 Finish like a regular Bowline—bring the running end down over the top and tuck it to exit parallel to the standing part.

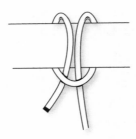

STEP 3 Another way to tie a Cow Hitch is by first passing a bight behind and back over the object, and then pulling both ends all the way through the bight.

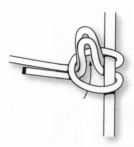

Another variation of the Cow Hitch is the Pedigree Cow Hitch—the difference is that you tuck the running end inside the turns for extra security. This hitch is secure enough to put tension on just the standing part.

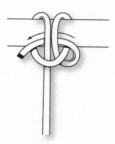

You can also tie the Cow Hitch in the bight by making opposing crossing turns and placing them together, leaving it ready to slide over an object.

Coxcombing

The most basic form of Coxcombing is known as French Whipping and is best tied with small string that helps keep a rope end from fraying. For three-strand Coxcombing, follow Steps 2 through 4.

STEP 1 To form French Whipping, make a set of continuous Half Hitches (see Chapter 4) around a bar or rail.

STEP 2 Seize three cords to a bar or rail, and start Half Hitches in alternating directions, as shown (see Appendix A for details on seizing).

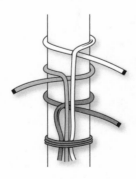

STEP 3 Continue by always taking the last cord used and making a Half Hitch in the direction opposite to the previous one.

STEP 4 Tighten each hitch as you go, and it will form a pattern similar to a Three-Strand Braid along its length.

Coxcombings are generally made as protective coverings or over handles or rails to provide a better grip. Other "whippings" to protect rope ends are shown in Appendix A.

Crown Sennit

The Crown Sennit is based on a series of Crown Knots (see Chapter 1), but with four strands instead of three. To begin, bind four cords or ropes together, with tape or a Constrictor Knot (see Chapter 6) tied in string.

STEP 1   Form the first Crown Knot, as shown.

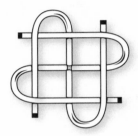

STEP 2   Tighten the first knot, and make another one.

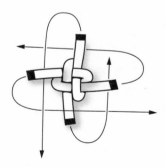

STEP 3 Tighten the second knot on top of the first one and continue tying Crown Knots, one on top of the other.

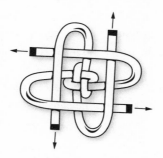

STEP 4 Repeat the Crown Knots until the sennit reaches desired length.

Ocean Plait Braid

Use the Ocean Plait Braid to make a floor or table mat. Old ropes may be retired to serve as material for these mats. To make an Ocean Plait mat, you'll need a longer length of rope than you think, especially if you plan to triple or quadruple the pattern to make the mat larger.

STEP 1 Start by making a right-handed Overhand Bend (see Chapter 2) and lay it on a flat surface with the ends of the rope pointed upward.

STEP 2 Pull down both bights of the Overhand and twist each once to the left, forming two crossing turns. Pull the left crossing turn over to the right, and then pull the left side of the right crossing turn through the left crossing turn.

STEP 3 Bring down each end and weave it through the mat to give the finished over-and-under pattern.

STEP 4 The ends should be interwoven as shown.

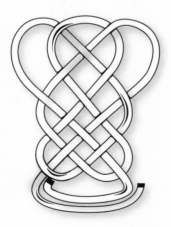

It might take a little practice to keep the pattern symmetrical. As you weave the rope, check that the crossings always alternate over and under, never crossing under or over twice consecutively, unless of course the pattern is doubled. The ends can either be seized (see Appendix A) or sewn in place.

Three-Strand Braid

The most common use for this braid is for braiding hair. However, it's also a good way to tie three lengths of rope into a single braided rope for more strength.

STEP 1 To start, you'll need three cords. The cords may simply be held together, or you can tie them together at the top. To start braiding, move the left cord to cross over the middle cord.

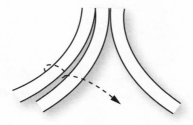

STEP 2 Next, take the right cord and cross it over the new middle cord.

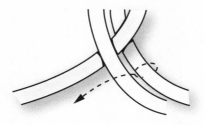

STEP 3 Continue making crossovers, alternating sides until the braid is as long as you need it to be. Secure the ends, if necessary.

The Three-Strand Braid is sometimes tied with strands of different colors. Moreover, each strand can be a pair of cords, or a group of cords.

TURK'S HEAD

This knot is known as a three-lead four-bight Turk's Head because it makes three turns around the bar and each rim has four bights. It can be tied over the hand or around a cylindrical object. If tightened, the Turk's Head can serve as a binding. To use this knot in making a mat, widen one of the rims while pushing the other to the center, making the knot flat.

STEP 1 Pass the running end twice around the bar, then over and under as shown by the arrow.

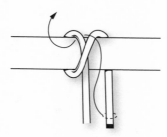

STEP 2 Flip the right crossing over the left one.

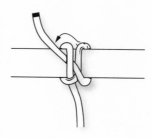

STEP 3   Thread the running end through the right crossing.

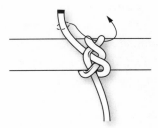

STEP 4   To double the knot, bring the running end around the back to the original start and follow the same pattern, staying next to the cord you are doubling without crossing over it.

When you tie the Turk's Head, you are braiding in a circle, so it helps to rotate it toward you as you proceed.

ROPE GROMMET

To make the Rope Grommet, use a single strand of natural fiber rope that has been unlayed but retains its spiral shape. Use a length about three and a half times the circumference of the Grommet you want to make.

STEP 1   Make a circle out of the center section, and start wrapping one of the ends just as you would start a Multiple Overhand Knot.

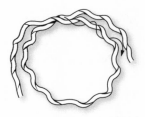

STEP 2   Continue these wraps, following the natural spiral shape of the strands, all the way around the circle. At this point, it should look like a ring of three-strand rope with one strand missing.

STEP 3 Now use the other end to fill in the place of the missing strand. Twisting it slightly as you go may help it seat better. Finish by tying the two ends in a Half Knot, just as you would in the first part of a Reef Knot (see Chapter 6), and then tuck the ends over and under the strands in the manner of the Back Splice (see Chapter 1).

Making Rope Grommets can help you better understand the structure of three-strand rope. Because synthetic rope tends to forget its shape when unlayed, it is awkward to use for making a Grommet.

Appendix A

COILING ROPE

Everything you do with rope—from selection and coiling to using it and deciding when to retire it—falls under the category of rope management.

The most important rope management skill is simple: using ropes properly. Tying knots that jam can damage the fibers of rope, and even more damage will result from having to pry a jammed knot apart. Tying hitches that are adjustable can aid in keeping slack out of the rope and can help prevent stress damage from shock loading. And, of course, ropes fare much better when they are properly matched to the application.

Many activities that use specific knots and ropes also have their own methods of rope care and management. For example, those who use ropes for climbing or rescue usually take great care not to step on them. Because the rope structure consists of a central core surrounded by a stiff outer layer, this core can take damage from a boot heel that will not be noticeable. Also, fishermen store fishing line away from direct sunlight to protect it from ultraviolet radiation, which might result in premature line weakness.

Much of the rope work methodology we use today was perfected on sailing ships. For centuries, operating a square-rigged sailing vessel required an army of men plying their craft with rope. Because their principal tool for working with rope was the marlinespike, this craft became known as "marlinespike seamanship," and this term is still used today.

Sometimes it is more challenging to store rope than to use it. The best way to store rope is by wrapping the entire length into a coil and tying a part of itself around the coil to keep it secure. When rope turns into a tangle, it's annoying, but what's worse is that it will get twisted, with very sharp turns or kinks. These can damage rope fibers, making it much weaker. Coiling rope is also helpful because rope can be dangerous under foot when loose, especially on boats.

You can coil the rope by reaching for each new length with the right hand and adding it to the coil held in the left hand. Stiffer or more tightly laid rope will have more of a tendency to twist into a figure-eight shape than looser rope will. To counteract this tendency, try giving the rope a right-hand twist with each turn of the coil. As you reach out your right hand and grip the rope with your palm away from you, twist your hand and the rope as if you were turning a screwdriver to tighten a screw. Even if you're left-handed, you should still coil them in a clockwise direction because most three-stranded ropes are twisted in a right-handed direction.

If the rope is stiff enough to make even figure eights, then skip the twists and store it as a bundle of that shape. Starting with the first end hanging down lower than the bottom of the coil will help keep it from getting caught in the turns, which can cause the rope to tangle as you uncoil it.

As you have seen in many cases throughout this book, you don't always need the end of a rope in order to make a knot. This is also the case when tying the finishing knot on the coils shown in this chapter. It may be that you need to coil up rope that is in service, and the ends are tied to something, as is often the case on a sailboat. In the case of the Gasket Coil, you can start wrapping from the one free end and then make the final knot "in the bight." You can do this with the Figure-of-Eight Coil, also illustrated in this chapter. Many other knots can be made to secure a coil, and people often make up their own way of finishing the coil with the knot of their choice.

Large coils are sometimes bound with several small cords, called "stops," at intervals around the coil. When a rope is stored on a spool, the spool should turn as rope is being taken from it at a 90-degree angle from the turning axis of the spool. If the spool is laid on end with the rope pulled up over one end, each turn will result in a twist in the rope, which can result in kinks. When a coil is bound in the middle as in the case of the Gasket Coil, it is sometimes called a "hank."

METHODS OF PREVENTING FRAYING

Caring for rope includes taking care of the ends. Ropes are made of many fibers and strands that will separate quickly if not secured. If synthetic three-strand rope is cut without preparation, the three strands will unravel for several feet in just a moment. Other ropes, whether braided or plaited, also unravel or become frayed. The end must be bound in some way, and there are a number of ways to accomplish this.

One way to stop the end of a rope from becoming frayed is to make a binding with string near the end. When this binding consists of many wraps it is called a "whipping," probably named thus because on square-riggers a rope end that was loose would "whip" around in the wind. One way to make this kind of binding is with the Coxcombing (shown in Chapter 11). Two additional methods are illustrated in this chapter. In general, it is best to use natural fiber binding string on natural fiber ropes, and synthetic material on synthetic ropes.

Anything that binds the end of a rope will help stop it from fraying or becoming unraveled, and there are many options. The quickest way is to tie a stopper knot. Even an Overhand Knot will help, although it makes for a bulky solution. For three-strand rope, the Back Splice (see Chapter 1) will make a nice-looking end, but it's somewhat bulky as well. If you have string but don't have time to make a proper whipping, a Constrictor Knot (see Chapter 6) makes a good temporary binding.

Many people rely on a butane lighter to bind their rope end. Partially melting the rope's end to keep it from fraying is jovially called the Butane Back Splice. After a knot is tied and the running end is cut close, some people like to burn the tip, making it swell in size so that it's less likely to pull back into the knot. When burning the tip, it's important not to let the flame weaken the knot. Stores that sell rope sometimes have a cutting hot wire that leaves the ends heat-sealed after cutting.

However, using a flame only works for synthetic ropes. Heat will not seal the ends of natural fiber ropes because the fibers scorch and burn without melting. Thus, a lighter can also be used to help determine if a rope is natural or synthetic. The only exception to this is Kevlar rope, which scorches without melting.

Yet another way to bind a rope end is with adhesive tape. When needed, different colors can be used to distinguish different ropes, and the tape can serve as a writing surface for labeling them. Or you can use heat shrink tubing and liquid plastic dip.

When you choose a binding method, keep in mind that some serve an additional purpose. Stiffening the end aids in threading the rope through a decorative knot, much like the plastic tip on shoelaces helps to thread the tip through the eyelets set in the shoes.

Seizing

A seizing is similar in form to Square Lashing as shown in Chapter 5, but is for lashing two ropes together. As shown previously, often an extra Half Hitch (see Chapter 4) is put in the running end after tying a knot to help make it secure. For increased security, a seizing can be used to anchor the running end to the standing end. This takes a little extra time but is very secure and can make a knotted attachment a permanent one.

In the Great Age of Sail, a hitch (or almost any knot, for that matter) was not considered permanent unless the running end was seized. Today, many people take pride in making a neatly wrapped coil or tying a whipping or seizing just right. The skills of rope management both use and complement many of the other skills of knotting with rope, and the methods that follow will certainly help round out your skills.

COMMON WHIPPING

You can use the following whipping technique to bind a rope's end.

STEP 1 Lay a crossing turn along the end of a rope and start making wraps, working inward.

STEP 2 Continue making wraps, and tuck the last wrap through the bight. Make sure the wraps are tightly side by side.

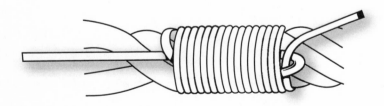

STEP 3 Tighten by pulling both ends, so that the crossing stays in the middle of the wraps.

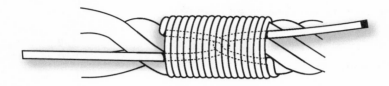

The length of the whipping should be at least as long as the diameter of the rope. If you are tying the whipping over three-strand rope, the direction of the wrapping should be opposite to the direction of the strands. The ends can be trimmed close or knotted together with a Reef Knot (see Chapter 6).

FIGURE-OF-EIGHT COIL

Start coiling the rope by folding it in half and making the turns with the doubled line, or by making the turns from one end to the other.

STEP 1   After wrapping all but the last two to four feet, depending on the size of the coil, fold a long bight in the end.

STEP 2   Pass this bight across the front and around behind the coil.

STEP 3 Pass the bight's end over itself and through the coil to the back.

After tying, you are left with a convenient bight that can be used to hang the coil over a nail or peg.

GASKET COIL

Also called the Buntline Coil, the Gasket Coil is often used to tie off excess line on a sailboat. Access to either end is not needed when finishing this coil, which means that the line used in the last tuck can be attached to the rigging.

STEP 1 After coiling the rope, pass one end several times around the middle of the coil.

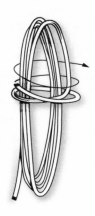

STEP 2   Pull a bight of the end through the top half of the coil and over the top.

STEP 3   Pull the bight down to the middle and take out any slack.

Seizing

For the following method, it's possible to use small string (also used for whipping). The following diagrams show larger rope for purposes of clarity.

STEP 1 Make a Constrictor Knot (see Chapter 6) around both ropes, leaving one end of the string long enough to make the seizing. Make many wraps for a distance of at least two rope diameters.

STEP 2 When the last wrap is made, tuck the string between the ropes and proceed to make exactly two frapping turns.

STEP 3   After exactly two frapping turns, make these tucks and then pull them down between the ropes.

Tighten the seizing by pulling the running end down between the ropes, until the last tucks you have made are tightly wedged between the ropes.

WEST COUNTRY WHIPPING

You can make this type of whipping at the end of a rope, or you can add it to a place on the rope where you plan to make the cut, so that you prevent the end from fraying.

STEP 1   Tie an Overhand Knot around the rope, leaving both ends of equal length.

STEP 2   Shift the ends to the opposite side and tie another Overhand Knot. Continue making knots, alternating sides, until you achieve a whipping of the right length.

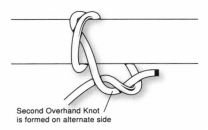

Second Overhand Knot is formed on alternate side

For variation, start the whipping with a Constrictor Knot and finish with a Reef Knot (see Chapter 6 for both) for added security.

GLOSSARY OF TERMS

AGE OF SAIL

The time period before steam engines, when ships large and small used mainly wind for locomotion.

BELAY

To secure a rope to an anchoring point; in rock climbing, to secure your position.

BEND

A knot for joining two ropes together at their ends.

BIGHT

A section of the rope often pulled to a tight curve to become part of a knot.

BIND

To seize, lash, or otherwise trap an object and its components.

BRAID

The interweaving of multiple strands.

CABLE-LAID ROPE

Three three-strand ropes twisted together to form a larger twisted rope.

CAPSIZED KNOT

A knot that underwent a change of form due to strain, usually when a curved part straightens, causing the shape of other components of the knot to change.

COIL

A rope that has been collected into a stack of crossing turns and (usually) secured with a knot, for storage.

CORDAGE

A general term referring to ropes and twines.

COXCOMBING

A continuous set of hitching of one or more strands to cover an object, usually bar shaped.

CROSSING KNOT

A knot made by one rope around another at the point where it crosses it, then continuing past it.

CROSSING TURN

A circle made of rope where the bases cross each other.

DOUBLE

To use two cords instead of one, laid parallel to each other.

EYE

A closed loop in rope, whether it is spliced, seized, or knotted.

FIBERS

The smallest threadlike components of cordage.

FID

A cylinder that is tapered to a point at one end, used for separating the lay of twisted rope when splicing.

FIXED LOOP

Also called a "locked loop," a fixed loop is a type of loop knot that does not allow the loop to change size, either by pulling on the standing part or the running end.

FRAPPING TURN

A wrap made across the middle of a set of turns already made for a lashing, used to tighten and secure them.

FRAYED

Unraveled, usually referring to the tip of a rope.

GUY LINES

Stays, or support lines that help secure tall objects, such as poles.

HALYARD

Name given to rope on a boat that raises and lowers sails.

HANK

A coil of rope that is secured at the middle with a number of wraps.

HAWSER

Refers to three-strand twisted rope; is a nautical term.

HITCH

A knot that fastens a rope to an object.

JAM

When a knot cannot be untied readily.

KINK

A tight turn in rope that can form when it has extra twists in it due to handling. It is damaging to the rope fibers.

KNOT

Any complication in rope that has the potential for the rope to act differently than if it were not there. Often refers to a structure that will remain in place under normal use.

LANYARD

A strap or short length of rope or braid that serves as a handle. It is generally made into a loop and is often used on tools to prevent their loss.

LARIAT

Also called a "lasso," it is a rope made into a slip loop, often used like a snare.

LASHING

Using multiple wraps and frapping turns to secure two or more poles together.

LEAD

Refers to the standing and running parts of the rope that exit from a finished knot. Also refers to their direction.

LEVERAGED TIE

A fastening or hitch that allows you to apply more tension on an object than you are exerting to tighten it.

LINE

How rope on a boat is referred to when in use.

LOOP KNOT

A knot that locks a section of rope into a circle or other closed form.

MARLINESPIKE

Similar to a fid and generally made of metal, it is also used as a grip for pulling twine tightly for seizings.

NAUTICAL

Pertaining to the sea or boats.

NOOSE

A slipped loop that is closed by pulling on the standing part.

PLAIT

A form of braid, making a rope of noncircular cross section, or flat braid.

REEVE

To pass a rope through the lead of a pulley or other tackle.

RIDING TURNS

A second set of turns, usually over a seizing, and having one less turn than the set beneath it.

ROPE

Cordage that is too large in cross section to be referred to as twine. It is generally made up of more than one strand or component.

ROUND TURN

When a rope is wrapped around an object such that it passes behind it twice.

RUNNING END

Also called the end, the working end, and the tag end; refers to the tip of the rope when used in forming a knot.

SEIZING

A form of lashing, used to secure one rope to another, often the running end back to the standing part, after the knot is formed.

SENNIT

Braided cordage, also called sinnet.

SHEATH

The part of a rope that forms its outer covering, when it has a "sheath and core" structure.

SHOCK LOADING

Placing temporary tension on a slack rope as it comes under sudden strain.

SLACK

When there is room to pull on a rope or knot, without tightening it.

SLING

A ready-made form of rope, usually a closed loop, that can readily be applied to something to serve as a hitch.

SLIP KNOT

A knot where the last tuck is made with the running end folded over into a bight, such that it can be released by just pulling on the running end.

SLIP NOOSE

A knot with a loop that closes down in size by pulling on the standing part; it can usually be completely untied by pulling the standing part all the way through.

SNUG

To take the slack out of a knot and tighten it.

SPILL

When a knot capsizes, loosens, or unties, either by accident or on purpose.

SPLICE

To fasten a rope to itself or another rope by interweaving the strands.

STANDING PART

Any part of the rope other than the running end that is not being used as a bight; it does not take part in forming the knot, but only takes strain.

STOPPER KNOT

Also called a "terminal knot," a type of knot tied at the end of a rope, usually for the purpose of preventing the rope from unreeving from something or to provide a better handhold.

STRAIN

Also called "tension," strain is the result of the rope performing the basic job that it does, transferring force.

STRAND

A small single cord, or the largest components of a rope.

STRENGTH

The amount of strain or tension that a rope can safely handle, or the amount it can take before breaking. When referring to a knot, it is how much that particular knot weakens a particular cordage when tied in it.

STRETCH

The property of rope to become longer under strain.

TIE

To form a knot from cordage, or to fasten cordage to something with a knot.

TIED IN THE BIGHT

Also called "in-the-bight"; refers to forming a knot without access to either end.

TURN

When a rope passes once around an object.

WHIPPING

Wrapping a string or twine repeatedly around a rope near the tip, to secure it from fraying.

YARN

Thin twine formed by twisting together a small group of fibers.

Appendix C

RESOURCES

BOOKS

Ashley, Clifford W. *The Ashley Book of Knots* (New York: Doubleday, 1993). This large, hardcover book is considered by many knot tyers as the "bible" on the subject.

Budworth, Geoffrey. *The Complete Book of Sailing Knots* (New York: The Lyons Press, 2000).

Budworth, Geoffrey. *The Ultimate Encyclopedia of Knots and Ropework* (London: Lorenz Books, 1999).

Fry, Eric C. *The Complete Book of Knots & Ropework* (Great Britain: David & Charles, 1994).

Graumont, Raoul, and John Hensel. *Encyclopedia of Knots and Fancy Rope Work.* 4th ed. (Centreville, Maryland: Cornell Maritime Press, 1994).

Leeming, Joseph. *Fun with String* (Toronto, Canada: Dover Publications, Inc., 1985).

Marino, Emiliano. *The Sailmaker's Apprentice* (Camden, Maine: International Marine, McGraw-Hill, 1994, 2001).

Merry, Barbara. *The Splicing Handbook.* 2nd ed. (Camden, Maine: International Marine, McGraw-Hill, 2000).

Miles, Roger E. *Symmetric Bends: How to Join Two Lengths of Cord* (Singapore: World Scientific Publishing, Co., 1995).

Newman, Bob, and Tami Knight. *Knots Around the Home* (Birmingham, AL: Menasha Ridge Press, 1997).

Pawson, Des. *The Handbook of Knots* (New York: DK Publishing, Inc., 1998).

Perry, Gordon. *Knots* (London: Barnes & Noble, Inc., 2002).

Smith, Bruce, and Allen Padgett. *On Rope North American Vertical Rope Techniques* (Huntsville, AL: National Speleological Society, Inc., 1996).

Toss, Brion. *The Complete Rigger's Apprentice* (Camden, Maine: International Marine, McGraw-Hill, 1997).

ORGANIZATIONS

The International Guild of Knot Tyers

www.igkt.net

The International Guild of Knot Tyers is an association of people with interests in knots and knotting techniques of all kinds. They have over 1,000 members worldwide from all walks of life, including academics, surgeons, sailors, athletes, scouters, magicians, farmers, miners, and accountants. Membership is open to anyone interested in knotting (whether expert or simply hoping to learn from others). They also publish a quarterly journal called *Knotting Matters*.

International Guild of Knot Tyers—North American Branch

www.igktnab.org

This is a sub-branch of the IGKT, formed in the Northeastern United States. They have biannual conventions for knot tyers to share their knowledge and learn from others.

International Guild of Knot Tyers–Pacific Americas Branch

www.igktpab.org

This chapter of the IGKT was formed in Southern California in January 1997 to bring a local focus for knotters in the Western United States, Canada, and Alaska.

WEBSITES WORTH VISITING

Knots on the Web

www.earlham.edu/~peters/knotlink.htm

The largest collection of knotting links on the Internet, this site even includes links to activities that use knotting extensively. However, some of the links are no longer active.

Ropers Knots Page

www.realknots.com

This site offers another extensive Internet knotting reference source.

INDEX